Musings on Plato's *Symposium*

ALEX PRIOU

Political Animal Press
www.politicalanimalpress.com
Distributed by the University of Toronto Press
www.utpdistribution.com

Cataloguing data available from Library and Archives Canada
ISBN: 9781895131673

Cover image adapted from "Plato's Symposium" (1648), an etching by Pietro Testa (1612–50).

Printed and bound in Canada

To Kristin,
for blessing me with two beautiful daughters,
Penelope and Tabitha

Contents

Preface

This book is decidedly *not* a work of scholarship, stubbornly not. It offers a holistic interpretation of Plato's *Symposium*, as is conventional among scholarly books, but departs by presenting it as a series of musings, beginning with the puzzles of the dialogue's various parts, long perplexing to me, and ascending therefrom in the direction of the whole. I have chosen this style because I am interested not so much in speaking to scholars as I am in guiding those similarly perplexed, those whose questions come from within and whose paths are their own, rather than those who take their bearings by the community of the learned, with their pre-existing concerns and themes. To such readers, then, for whom love has become a deep, *personal* problem, who are drawn therefore to the *Symposium* and enthusiastic for distilled reflections on this or that passage, distilled and for that reason, I hope, also thought-provoking—to them do I offer this little book. I have therefore written each section, so that it will be largely intelligible when read alone. Readers curious, however, about how the *Symposium* fits together as a whole would profit most by reading more or less straight through.

Such departures from scholarly convention occur much too rarely. Every act of interpretation, when so much as spoken, still worse when published, is something of a betrayal. For to say what an author has left unsaid is an indecent act of public stripping. Often an author is silent out of ignorance; in such cases, the exposure of his illness or deformity is justifiable at least in the name of public health. But when he has good reasons for not speaking, when he does so to make the reader complicit in the act of thinking, then to say aloud what he has passed over in pregnant silence is an offense not just to common decency but still worse to philosophy. It is a congenital defect of the scholar that he considers it his professional duty to expose; his unscrupulousness in adducing evidence for *what* he has exposed even makes one shudder. Or it would, were his methods not *de arte* ill-suited to the mode of writing employed by the philosophers, for rarely, all too rarely, does the scholar rise to the occasion and meet the philosopher on an equal plane. Nevertheless, practically speaking, such rare moments do nothing to alleviate the general tendency of the scholar, who in demanding that the philosophers' reasons be laid bare demands that his fellow scholars do the same, even more so. Whence the constant nods to the literature, the innumerable footnotes, the mile-long bibliographies. Whence also my stubbornness. Were this a book on Kant, I would be far more amenable to the demands of the scholar, close as they are to the philosopher's own mode and tendency. But in the case of Plato, such demands would be a cold shower, meant to bring you to your senses and cure you of the playful questioning, without which Plato refuses to let himself be stripped. And his *Symposium*? Two minutes at a "symposium" of scholars, with their PowerPoints and projectors, their handouts and convention centers, more than suffice to demonstrate how poorly their training prepares them to understand the amiable air and erotic fireworks at Agathon's house, to say nothing of Plato's strange mixture of the playful, prankish, flirtatious, outrageous, and beyond. It is obscene to unclasp a woman's bra in public; to fumble at it ineptly is a double shame, to pursuer and pursued alike.

For these reasons, I could not bring myself to write such a work on the *Symposium*. This book is therefore not a work of scholarship but a study, *properly* a study: a book written, in other words, *by* a student and *for* fellow students, *serious* students, be this their first frolic with the *Symposium* or only the latest in a long string of dalliances. It presumes, then, and reasonably enough, that its readers actually want to *think*; that when they open the book and see no survey of the literature, no attempt to situate the interpretation among the scholarship, they will not feel lost, nor will they feel slighted, but will allow the work to forge its way independently; that when they encounter a puzzle or question, or the occasional interruption from an unexpected interlocutor, they will not grow frustrated that no solution is proposed or speaker identified, but will search for themselves, whether in this book or in the text of the *Symposium* itself; that when it is claimed that the text says or does not say something, and this to their surprise, they will not be annoyed at the lack of citation, but will look to the text again, aware that the eye sees less than it would like to admit, a tendency helpfully corrected by the eye of another and gradually overcome by its looking back once again; and that when an assumption is made in one place, they will not cry foul, but seek either its support or its criticism, or even both, elsewhere in the book, even if only in passing. I have, in short, done what scholars seldom permit themselves to do: I have written a book I actually enjoyed writing and, I will admit, enjoy reading, too. It is my conviction that this enjoyment is the surest guide to that of my chosen reader. It is, at any rate, the only guide I have.

I have therefore seldom cited the text, save where I thought such citations would aid in thinking rather than take its place. I have still more rarely engaged the scholarship, lest I burden the text with tedious notes of the "so-and-so also notices" and "so-and-so has argued" variety. I should, however, acknowledge up front those works on Plato's *Symposium* that have inspired me throughout, Leo Strauss's *On Plato's* Symposium (University of Chicago Press, 2001) and Seth Benardete's "On Plato's *Symposium*," which can be found appended to his translation (University of Chicago Press, 2001). The *Symposium* was the first Platonic dialogue I ever read, and these the first commentaries. The interpretation here advanced has been developed in constant dialogue with both authors, in the decades since that initial encounter; those familiar with these works will see their influence at every turn, both where our paths converge and where they diverge. Hardly a word in it has escaped their influence.

For the Greek text of the *Symposium*, I have used the edition by Kenneth Dover (Cambridge University Press, 1980). All translations of this and other texts are my own; in preparing my translations of the *Symposium*, I have relied on the aforementioned translation by Seth Benardete.

Musings on Plato's *Symposium*

1. The Gathering

The *Symposium*—literally, the *Drinking Party*. Yet nobody in the dialogue seems to view the gathering that way. In the prologue, it's referred to once as a dinner and four times simply as a gathering, literally "being-together"; then, in the dialogue itself, it's initially referred to solely as a dinner; but, once the dining is done, there is an emphatic turn toward the subject of drinking, after which they make no further mention of this dinner.[1] The deliberation about drinking ends with the group deciding *not* to conduct the present gathering through intoxication but for each to drink as suits his pleasure, that it will rather be a gathering through *speeches*. They decide, in other words, that it will *not* be a symposium or drinking party, a decision implicitly acknowledged by those in the prologue, those relating the story after the fact. Why, then, did Plato call it *Symposium*, when only some drink and others abstain?[2] Why isn't it simply called the *Gathering*?

Plato may not have been referring to literal drinking; he may rather have had in mind a figurative or metaphoric intoxication, an intoxication not of the body but of the soul. The only person other than Plato to refer to the gathering as a drinking party is Alcibiades. The drunken Alcibiades confesses Socrates' powerful ability both to resist Alcibiades' charm and to charm him, in turn. Socrates easily resists the effects of drink and the effects of Alcibiades' beauty, if not also of beauty as such. Socrates is an island of sobriety amid a sea of intoxication: he criticizes the others for praising love or *erōs* by attaching to it the greatest and most beautiful things, true or not, when they ought instead to have spoken the truth about *erōs*—the beautiful truths, arranged attractively. The puzzle of the title may therefore be resolved thus: it is a warning not to grow too intoxicated with the dialogue's manifest beauty, a caution advising us instead to attend to Socrates and his peculiar sobriety, however intoxicating or mad he may at first appear. Alcibiades, at least, claims to have uncovered the naked truth of Socrates' hubris, of his philosophic mania and revelry: it is his *moderation*.

2. The Sicilian Expedition

There is great interest, even intrigue, about the gathering at Agathon's house. It took place in 416 BC, just prior to Athens' ill-fated invasion of Sicily, the so-called Sicilian Expedition. On the eve of the Athenians' departure, somebody mutilated the Herms about Athens, after which it also emerged that some time ago there had been a private party, where, in a fit of drunken playfulness, the attendees had mocked the sacred mysteries of Eleusis. Among those accused of this sacrilege was Alcibiades, who was for that recalled from his post co-leading the expedition, and so fled into the arms of Athens' then-enemy, Sparta. But that was many years before it was told, in the prologue. The prologue takes place after Alcibiades' return to Athens and his subsequent role leading the sacred procession to Eleusis, whose mysteries he had nearly a decade earlier been accused of profaning. I suspect that it takes place only after his death in 404.

The dialogue's theme grounds it in the events of the Peloponnesian War. Thucydides tells us that the Sicilian Expedition appealed to the Athenians' *erōs*, that it was the description alone, as opposed to the sight of it, that inflamed them. Some fifteen years prior, Pericles had first aroused their *erōs* during—of all things—a funeral oration, the solemnity of which offered him the opportunity to beautify Athens and thus steel the Athenians' resolve after the first year of the war, over and against their factious jealousies. Shortly thereafter, however, a plague hit Athens, and the Athenians' moral corruption was exposed; for this reason, Pericles was ultimately forced to concede that Athens was not the school of Greece but her tyrant. Thus began an overt policy of self-interest that forced Athens down an unseemly path; at the low point on that path, the Athenians naturally sought redemption, something they appeared to find in a vision of strength beautiful in the fear and trembling it produced, a beauty that might compensate for the ugliness of Athenian domination by divinizing it, making themselves "masters of the sea" and effectively putting Poseidon out of work. Such was the sight of the departing expedition to Sicily. Captivated by that sight, the Athenians blessed their fleet with a libation to the gods. Is there a connection between the Athenians' *erōs* for the expedition and the intoxication alluded to by the title *Symposium*, *Drinking Party*? The group's decision to praise *erōs* seems symptomatic of Athens' longing to redeem her tyrannical empire with a display of her power, a vision to replace the beauty of Periclean Athens, long since lost. If so, then Socrates' sobriety stands as an island in a vast, open sea of intoxication.

But what effect could his sobriety have had amid so much psychic inebriation? And isn't Socrates also surrounded by lovers, the most infamous being Alcibiades? Is Socrates really sober? His speech tells of the dizzying heights of erotic ambition, immediately after which the volatile and ambitious Alcibiades enters drunk and sings Socrates' praises! Perhaps the title is rather a warning against Socrates, as the peak of Athenian *décadence*. Would Plato then be a lover of Socrates' great critic, the comic poet Aristophanes?

3. The Love of Socrates

Let us say something about the love of Socrates. There are at least four such lovers in the dialogue. Two of them offer us our first glimpse of love in this work, Plato's dialogue on love. They are Apollodorus and Aristodemus. Aristodemus was present at the original conversation, and he told it to Phoenix and Apollodorus, both of whom told it to Glaucon, perhaps the brother of Plato immortalized in the *Republic*. With the possible exception of Phoenix, all are associates of Socrates. The original conversation seems to have circulated for some time among these Socratics, that is, among lovers of Socrates and of philosophy. Apollodorus is a more recent addition to this cohort, and his love of Socrates, along with the apparent safety, now that Alcibiades is back and forgiven, if not also dead, has led him to speak more freely of this conversation than would have been advisable in the intervening years. For there can be little doubt that what Alcibiades reveals about his relationship with Socrates is not only embarrassing for him but likely damaging to Socrates. At least it would be, if it got out beyond Socrates' coterie, to those not so devoted to Socrates and philosophy.—Yet it does!, thanks to Apollodorus, who's the sort of lover happy to tell stories about his beloved to any willing audience, even those for whom he has contempt, the unnamed moneymakers and non-philosophers he regales with the story of the *Symposium*.[3] Do Apollodorus' loose lips sink Socrates' ship? If so, then it is a dark, ironic turn that he cries throughout Plato's *Phaedo*, for he would himself have been responsible for the death of his god, Socrates.[4] Perhaps he even cries because he knows this himself and is wracked with guilt.

I suggested that Apollodorus is the sort of lover to deify his beloved; it's for this reason that he looks down on everyone else, himself included. He could never imagine his beloved Socrates stooping to love him back. So, as the comrade observes, philosophy has not made him happy but rather miserable. Aristodemus, on the other hand, is the sort of lover who imitates his beloved, who sees him as a model on which to base his own conduct. But while Aristodemus can imitate Socrates' attire, going shoeless, he can't drink as much, nor can he stay up as late—he certainly can't speak as well. Both lovers are therefore ridiculous. Plato portrays Socrates' lovers comically. But what did Socrates think of them? Socrates invites Aristodemus to the dinner at Agathon's house, only to drop back in silent thought, so that Aristodemus is forced to arrive alone. Adding to this bit of rudeness, Socrates also arrives late to dinner, only to make an ironic jest at his patient and gracious host's expense—a jest Agathon notices and won't soon forget. Is Socrates' abandonment of Aristodemus, like his jest at Agathon, a bit of cruel humor on his part, a prankish joke? Perhaps. Plato, at least, must have found it funny.

4. Eros and Dialectics

Apollodorus and Aristodemus are Plato's playful personification of the twofold character of *erōs* as deifying and thus separating, on the one hand, and as modeling and thus combining, on the other. That is, they personify *sunkrisis* and *diakrisis*, which come together in the quintessential Socratic activity of dialectics or conversation, *to dialegesthai*.[5] In its erotic context, however, this activity centers on the question whether the proper end of *erōs* is the self-negating vision of the perfect God, on the one hand, or the self-affirming articulation of the good life for man as man, on the other. Does Plato ever answer this most serious of questions?

5. Socrates the Beautiful and Good

Aristodemus encounters Socrates washed and properly clothed, quite strange given his typically Spartan attire. Though Apollodorus doesn't say so, Socrates must have looked ridiculous, like a homeless man with his unkempt hair washed and parted, wearing a tux and holding a bouquet of flowers. Socrates seems in on the fun, though: in a self-deprecating joke, he says, "Beautiful I go to a beauty." That beauty is Agathon, and just a moment later, as a way of encouraging Aristodemus to go uninvited to Agathon's house, he plays on Agathon's name, saying, "The good (*agathoi*) go of their own accord to the feasts of the good (*agathōn*)." Socrates says both he and Agathon are both beautiful and good, but is this anything more than a joke, than merely playful speech? Socrates, who never tires of speaking of the good, has made himself beautiful—or rather has made himself ridiculous in trying to be beautiful. Conversely, Agathon the beautiful is in name good, but perhaps *only* in name. Socrates, and Plato with him, playfully suggests that the attempt to beautify the good risks producing something ridiculous, while the beautiful may be only nominally good. Let's not forget that Socrates' speech, as we will see, collapses the two beautifully, and that it does so both through the sin of omission and by virtue of Platonic poetry. What *is* their relationship?

Another thing. When speaking of the good, Socrates quotes Homer, whom he accuses of arrogance in having the lesser Menelaus go uninvited to the tent of his superior, Agamemnon. Socrates ignores, however, that the men are brothers. Shouldn't the affection of a great man for his own brother, for his flesh and blood, moderate his love of the good and the beautiful?

6. Agathon's House

The atmosphere at Agathon's house is nothing if not genial. When Aristodemus arrives, he is ushered into the dinner, where Agathon greets him graciously and with open arms, even though he wasn't invited. Agathon is a true Athenian gentleman (*kalokagathos*) in his easy and accommodating social graces, a virtue that has the merit of saving the poor, abandoned Aristodemus from otherwise unavoidable embarrassment. Everything is open and free, from start to finish, with servants dining alongside guests and host, as though equals, and with guests coming and going as they please.[6] It's all quite lovely.

Yet the urgent manner in which Aristodemus is ushered in suggests a curious lack of freedom in one crucial respect, a lack of freedom to abstain. After greeting Aristodemus, Agathon asks where Socrates is, and when he learns that he's on the neighbor's porch, he sends his slaves back out after him. Aristodemus protects Socrates from Agathon's repeated attempts to bring him in—he protects Socrates' *freedom*. Not everyone is so eager to join the free and easy atmosphere of Agathon's dinner party, then. Socrates will come, to be sure, but only when he is good and ready; in the meantime, his temporary abstention requires that Aristodemus defend him from the party's host.

But there's another intriguing possibility. Did Agathon's slaves usher Aristodemus in so quickly because they were on strict orders to rush Socrates in, and because Aristodemus matched their master's description of the man himself? "He's dirty, shoeless, and ugly—trust me, you can't miss him!" So perhaps the party's atmosphere isn't so liberal, after all. When Socrates arrives, he makes a joke at Agathon's expense, to which Agathon responds by playfully threatening to take him to court. Perhaps this is Plato's little reminder that the principal accuser to get Socrates killed was Meletus, a poet. What's Agathon's problem?

7. The Gathering Deliberates

With the planned dinner done, the gathering turns to the serious matter of drinking. Initially, Pausanias takes lead of the deliberation, asking the others whether they're up for a second round after the rager the night before. Aristophanes, an otherwise capable drinker, first speaks up and readily declines, citing yesterday evening's baptism. Meanwhile, the doctor Eryximachus listens on and, upon Aristophanes' response, jumps in, taking the lead from Pausanias by revealing that he needs to hear from only one other person, Agathon, who likewise declines. Evidently, Eryximachus has already heard from the rest—Aristodemus, Phaedrus, and some others who go unnamed. But he didn't consult Socrates, an apparently rude oversight that the good doctor deems excusable, thanks to Socrates' well-known flexibility when it comes to drinking. The group therefore agrees that each may drink as he pleases. The gathering will therefore not be a drinking party, a symposium. Despite being excluded from the deliberation, Socrates raises no objection.

What, then, will it be? There will be *speeches*, concludes Eryximachus; but for speeches one needs a topic, so he requests the others permit him to make a proposal, and, upon their approval, he proposes that they give speeches in praise of Eros: Love, the *god* Love. This idea is not his but has its most immediate parentage in Phaedrus, who has evidently complained to Eryximachus many times before that none of the poets has written a hymn in praise of so great and so important a god. Socrates, the member of the group denied a say in the first deliberation, now takes over and decides the matter entirely on his own, speaking not only on his own behalf but on behalf of Agathon, Pausanias, and Aristophanes, as well, despite not having consulted with them yet, as Eryximachus had the decency to do. Socrates' presumptuousness is quite boorish, even arrogant, or rather it would have been, had all the others not immediately agreed and urged the same.—

For those charmed by the genial and genteel atmosphere at Agathon's house, by its liberal and amiable air, these two deliberations should be disheartening, as twice the established air of friendship almost vanishes, owing first to Eryximachus' presumptuousness and second to that of Socrates. Peace prevails, to be sure, but only thanks to the consent, whether voiced or not, of those ignored in each deliberation. So what guarantee is there that order will be maintained? It's easy to point the finger at Socrates as the real culprit here, seeing that he's the one who risks upsetting the unanimity of both deliberations. Socrates' presence could well spoil everything, so taxing is he of the flexible Agathon's ability to accommodate his guests. First, he shows up late, which may explain why Eryximachus didn't consult him—he may not have had time. Next, he insults his host, Agathon. Then, as we just saw, he takes singular control of the deliberations, arrogantly presuming himself qualified to speak on behalf of everyone else. Worse than that, when eventually it's his turn to speak, he will complain about how the others have praised *erōs* and so refuse to speak at all, unless the terms of the agreement be changed or refined—even though *he* was the one who rushed the inadequate second deliberation. And while the others do readily acquiesce to Socrates' special requests, when eventually he does speak it is for far longer than anyone else. What wouldn't have gone more smoothly, had Socrates not been there, at all?

Smoother, sure—but better? No. Socrates will eventually complain that the others praised *erōs* hyperbolically, attributing to it the greatest and most beautiful things, even when alien to it. By granting his special requests, the others allow Socrates to inject some much-needed sobriety into the conversation. Lament that Socrates is there? We ought to lament much more that Socrates didn't exert still greater control over this community, that he had to dilute his appearance, his speech, his whole manner in approaching these Athenians.

(Another puzzle: Eryximachus alludes to a conversation he may have had with Aristodemus about drinking, but Aristodemus doesn't include it in his narration. Eryximachus's remark is no doubt necessary to the narration. But why doesn't Aristodemus report the conversation itself? One possibility: as Socrates' lover, he looks away from himself and his own conversations to those of Socrates. A related puzzle: Did Aristodemus give a speech in praise of love? If so, then why doesn't he report it? And if not, why not?)

8. Praising Love

The group assigns itself the task of praising love, a task that no poet thus far has ever assumed for himself. Strange to think, too, considering how many of our songs, our movies, both tragic and comic, how many of our novels and poems have as their theme *love*. But a quick glance at any one of these suffices to show how we really view love. How many of these novels and poems are about love lost, about the often-insurmountable obstacles to attaining the goods love promises? We can pass over the tragedies readily, as their genre alone betrays the conclusions their authors draw. And though we appear saved from the tragic view by the genre of romantic comedies, which do in the end tend to praise love, still they only ever do so in the *end*, that is, by relying on the familiar trope of love found, love lost or jeopardized, then love regained—they succeed, that is, only by acknowledging and incorporating the *problems* of love. Much stranger it seems, then, that the group decides to *praise* it! So, is there not every danger that they will ignore the great risks that come with love? At the very least, their efforts might and indeed *do* aid in clarifying the critique of love, they *force* its critics to state with greater clarity what had until this point remained, for the most part, only implicit in the plots of the poets—they force a philosophic critique of the power and effect of *erōs* on the human soul.

9. Phaedrus' Speech

What wouldn't lovers do for their beloveds! Phaedrus, having many lovers himself, knows all-too-well their generosity; he also knows what makes them give: shame. To be sure, Phaedrus says that not just shame but also honor motivates the lover, and not just the lover but also the beloved. But he's just playing hard to get. The beloved places terms and conditions on the lover, he demands that his lover act honorably, lest he withhold from the lover what he wants in return. By favoring the honorable among his lovers, or rather those among his lovers who do honorable things, the beloved shows that he himself is also a lover, but a lover of honor, while his lovers, both successful and unsuccessful, can at best feel shame at doing anything that might meet with a disapproving and knowing look from their beloved, at anything that might cost them their beloved's reciprocation. But would such a beloved ever say what Phaedrus says? He would indeed be demanding, but without being altogether aware of, or at least open about, such erotic economics, to say nothing of generalizing them into an explicit strategy. But that's just what Phaedrus does, he generalizes the implicit but undisclosed strategy of the beloved. Phaedrus is the beloved become self-aware, the *mercenary* beloved. His longtime lover Eryximachus is, after all, a doctor.

Phaedrus' mercenary understanding of love leads him to the ultimate test of a lover's generosity, to the ultimate gift or sacrifice: death. How much, he wonders, is a lover willing to give? What would it take for the lover to give it all away, even life and all its goods? In what circumstances, what world, could such a sacrifice satisfy the lover's deepest longing, his *erōs*? Phaedrus doubts, I think, that the negative motivator—shame before the beloved—could ever transform into the love of honor, at least on its own. It would require something else, something neither lover nor beloved could bring to the negotiating table. It could only come from beyond the world of human affairs, from the gods. Only divine punishment and divine reward could compensate for the lover's loss of life. For with the loss of life, the lover also loses the one thing needful in his eyes: reciprocation, consummation, gratification. Orpheus was unwilling to die for his beloved, so the gods punished him by robbing him of his chance to live with her; and Alcestis was willing to die for her beloved, so the gods rewarded her by returning her to life, a life with her beloved. Absent the gods, however, Alcestis could not be understood as at bottom loving her husband but only as loving honor. Orpheus is the true image of the lover. For what the lover wants is not a noble death but a happy life. Phaedrus appeared, as the mercenary beloved, rather contemptible in his transactional *erōs*; but he gets his revenge, since in his speech the lover emerges as no less transactional than he.

Phaedrus goes further, however. He closes by praising Achilles, here presented as the self-sacrificing beloved. On his account, only the beloved is capable of an unmercenary love, only he can die selflessly, for all that he would love is honor. Phaedrus may not be such a beloved, but his speech reveals an important truth: the beloved, the object of love, is necessarily higher in rank than the lover. We could say more here, but better at another time; for now, one need only compare the tone of his speech, the speech of a beloved, with the tone of Pausanias' speech, that of a lover. Whereas Phaedrus presents the edifying image of a city of lovers and beloveds fighting valiantly alongside one another, Pausanias attempts to legitimize his sexual urges by passing them off as somehow necessary to "philosophy." The beloved's demands are inherently higher in dignity than the lover's compensation.—

What was Phaedrus up to, then, in asking the group to praise love? Why would he do such a thing, when there's every indication that he views the beloved as higher than the lover? Or did he rather propose this topic not so much as a request but as a challenge? And is this one of those prankish demands that the beautiful enjoy making of their lovers?

10. The Missing Speeches

After Phaedrus, some others speak, but Aristodemus could not remember them. Who were these speakers? We know, at least, that they did not speak critically of *erōs*, since Pausanias says that he is the first to do so. Nor could they have been particularly noteworthy as individuals, since no one ever mentions one of these speakers by name—But what about Aristodemus? He's mentioned, but we never hear him speak. And surely he'd remember his own speech, if he gave one, wouldn't he? Maybe he didn't even give a speech. But then why not? We know he's sitting next to Eryximachus, and thus between him and either Aristophanes or Agathon. My guess is that he's sitting between Eryximachus and Agathon and that he's skipped accidentally in the change in speaking-order that occurs thanks to Aristophanes' hiccups. But that just raises a further question: Why is little Aristodemus so easily forgotten? Why are the others able, even eager to "overlook" him? Is it because he's a poor imitation of Socrates, not worth much consideration on his own, especially since Socrates himself—the "original"—is present? Is it because the group is eager to hear Agathon speak, so that when Aristophanes has finished all turn past Aristodemus to the party's celebrated host? But then why doesn't Aristodemus speak up for himself? Is it because he wasn't invited and doesn't want to impose? Or is it because he, too, is eager to hear Socrates speak, after Agathon? Or maybe Aristodemus *did* give a speech, but chose to pretend he didn't, after hearing Socrates speak. Much of Socrates' speech corrects those who spoke before him; these parts are elenctic or refutative in character. Are the apparently non-elenctic parts of Socrates' speech latently elenctic, directed against speakers whose speeches are missing? And is Aristodemus among them?—Consider Aristophanes' "self-correction" at 193d8–e2, if it's even Aristophanes'.

11. Parmenides and Hesiod

Though according to Phaedrus no poet so far has hymned Eros, that doesn't mean there's been total silence about him. Phaedrus quotes two of his predecessors, Hesiod the poet and the philosopher Parmenides, primarily to show that they agree that Eros is among the oldest of the gods. But the verses he quotes show much more, especially when read in their original contexts. Parmenides fits Eros into an intelligently devised plan, whereas Hesiod relates that Eros came into being reason and purpose unknown, only thereafter to prove responsible for deceiving gods and men alike. We are made to wonder whether the world supports our deepest longings, whether by loving we find our place in the world, the *intelligible* world, or rather fall prey to "beautiful evils" sent by the gods. Is the intellect the friend or enemy of love? What follows?

12. Pausanias' Speech

Pausanias gives us the creeps—how could he not! with his wholly unsubtle attempt to justify his pedophilic urges, sublimated and ergo romanticized as an "education" of the budding intellect, of the mind in its initial protuberance. He speaks at length, longer than anyone else, save Socrates. Yet his speech is tediously belabored, the length unnecessary—or rather *absolutely* necessary, lest he fail to obfuscate his intention sufficiently to ennoble his...deeds.

Pausanias' basic position is so obviously convoluted as to be a caricature of the practice he promotes, though it's a caricature true to form, mind you. Every deed, he argues, is morally neutral; it is rather the manner in which it is done that provides the grounds for evaluation. For that one must look first to whether it is the body or the soul that the lover seeks, and for *that* one need only look to whether the lover is willing to stick around, to put in the time. The base lover wants the body in its present bloom, until its inevitable wane, while the noble lover wants the soul in its emerging and ever-developing beauty.—Now, there's an obvious problem with this, for if the noble lover is concerned with the beloved's soul, then why must they have sex? Why isn't the relationship wholly educational? What would such a relationship even look like? If not the body, and the specific demands, conventional or not, that this particular body makes of its lover, then what in this case would supply the criterion of selection? Would it not be the intellect alone, in its initial awakening, in the aforementioned self-aware ignorance and wonder before the basic perplexities?—But to return to Pausanias, the distinction between base and noble love appears now not so much as a distinction between the base and noble *lover* but as a distinction between the lover's base love of the body and the beloved's noble love of virtue. A hierarchy thus emerges, with sex at the lowest end and education in virtue at the higher end. But this is all against Pausanias' will, who hides his desires behind the euphemistic language of "favors," "gratification," and "assistance." We all know what you need "assistance" with, Pausanias, we've all seen it depicted on the vases!, have we not? (See the rendering on the opposite page.)[7] Ultimately, Pausanias is just a cowardly man seeking legal justification for his suspect longings, as a means to popular acceptance, and it has long been the habit of soft men like Pausanias to disguise their cowardice as moderation. By his own admission, he differs from base lovers only by his self-restraint, so he is every bit as attracted to the mindless beauties as base lovers are. So that one shudders to think how he'd act, had he been raised amid the more lax customs in Elis or among the Boeotians!—"Look, Pausanias may give you the creeps, but is your critique really specific to *his* sexual proclivities? Doesn't it apply to anyone who loves both the body and the soul of his beloved?" Very true, and all to the good.

13. Eryximachus' Speech

Eryximachus uses his speech to venerate his art, medicine. For that, however, he must claim that art as such is capable of the most far-reaching control, that it can master the whole of nature—"in short, everything there is." That's a tall order for technology even in our day, certainly in *his*, a time when medical school consisted in a four-year education, followed of course by internship and residency, in "cutting and burning," that is, amputation and cauterization, and without the philanthropic aid of our anesthesia. We are not inclined to take his veneration seriously, primitive as his art is; he is, we might say, exemplary not of *all* times but of *his* time alone. Eryximachus strikes us as a quaint predecessor, much as the amphibian frog might look back with a mixture of appreciation and pity on his legless and merely aquatic ancestor, the fish.—"Why, then, take seriously Plato's critique of this early devotee of technology? If Eryximachus' art is of merely historical interest, aren't those who take him seriously equally damned to contemporary irrelevance, your beloved Plato included?" It would be wrong, even fatally wrong, to assume that the antiquated *results* of Eryximachus' art prove it to be antiquated in every respect. Antiquated in ability? Yes. Antiquated in methods? Sure. But antiquated in intention? Hardly—rather, all *too* contemporary. And it is primarily against Eryximachus' far-reaching intention that Plato directs his critique. The silly arrogance of a man of such primitive abilities to lay claim to such far-reaching mastery is tangible and surely part of Plato's comic caricature. Less obvious is that, for all our progress in the technological mastery of nature, still our arrogance has diminished not an iota less; it has rather hardened into an adamantine conviction.—What, then, is the substance of Plato's critique? Eryximachus venerates art by laying claim to the technological mastery of nature, yet *twice* encounters limits to the power of art. Like Pausanias, Eryximachus identifies two forms of Eros, a noble and a base form. Art focuses on the noble form, understanding which desires should be gratified, which not. Medicine does this with bodies, filling and emptying them *not* according to the bad and sickly desires but according to what medicine dictates as nutritious, curative, therapeutic, pharmaceutic, etc. Beyond medicine and the human body, Eryximachus mentions the musical art, the art that Aristophanes, Agathon, and others possess, how music does the same as medicine but with notes, producing harmony, consonance, agreement, that is, the friendship of lovers. Here, though, Eryximachus hits a roadblock, admittedly: harmony exists not just in strings playing notes but has an inherent structure, an abstract constitution, which admits of no deviation from the correct order—there exists in this realm no base desires but merely a beautiful being. Not art, then, but science is highest here—science as pure contemplation, contemplation of being in itself, rather than in relation to human beings and their desires, both errant and correct, noble and base. But then where else, besides music? Are there other wholly beautiful beings, beyond technical manipulation? And what if not? Is art then higher than contemplation? Or is contemplation higher than art, even when contemplation of what is not beautiful, of what is ugly? But what art do we rely on, beyond music, what art is highest, governing "everything there is"? Eryximachus answers: divination, *prophecy*. This is an art, a technical ability? This is the peak of the technological mastery of nature? Is this not rather the shame of science, a humbling, humiliating admission that not all of being admits of comprehension, or rather falls under its control? Must not Eryximachus, and those among us today who share his intention, even as we outstrip his accomplishments, admit that being is a mystery, near the center of which is man? Beyond Eryximachus' veneration of art we thus find two superior not-artisans, non-technologists: the disinterested, theoretical contemplator of being and the pious adherent or interpreter of the will of the mysterious God.—"But which of these two peaks is the highest?"

14. Hiccups

Eryximachus uses his speech to venerate his art, medicine. For that, however, he must ignore the very base things with which medicine deals. Like Pausanias, Eryximachus hides his base concerns with euphemistic language. He speaks of "repletion and evacuation," but we all know what he means: medical treatments like emetics, diuretics, and laxatives—or, to be more precise, their successful effects: puking, pissing, and shitting. Even today a doctor treating a patient suffering from harmful gut bacteria might prescribe, so as to restore him to a healthy gut flora, pills containing the desirable bacteria, made from or even containing *human feces*. So, while to the man on the street "Eat shit!" would be considered an insult, to an Eryximachus that's just sound medical advice. Aristophanes' hiccups, and the treatment—gargling and sneezing—that Eryximachus prescribes, only scratch the surface of the baseness and filth with which medicine deals, but the surface alone suffices to expose the flaw at the heart of his speech, those facts that don't admit of technical understanding, what Leo Strauss calls "funny facts." They require instead a comic poet.—

After Aristophanes' hiccups are cured, each of the remaining speakers will present love in light of the low, even those who draw emphatic attention to its exalted heights: for Aristophanes, love is rooted in our necessary incompleteness; for Agathon, he is a beautification of the goddesses Necessity and Deception; and for Socrates, it is in *nearly* every case, if not finally in *every* case, a failed escape from death.

15. Aristophanes' Speech

What can I say about this most memorable, most beautiful, most plainly and commonly edifying speech in the *Symposium*? Listen to the powerful testimony of Allan Bloom:

> Plato makes Aristophanes the expositor of *the truest and most satisfying account* of Eros that we find in the *Symposium*. There has probably never been a speech or poem about love that so captures what men and women actually feel when they embrace each other. Both the myth and the reasons that underlie it give a beautiful justification for taking love seriously, and this speech has the advantage of being much more comprehensive than the others in dealing with *all species* of love. To say, "I feel so powerfully attracted and believe I want to hold on forever because this is my lost other half," gives word to what we actually feel and seems to be sufficient. It does not go beyond our experience to some higher principle, which has the effect of diluting our connection to another human being, nor does it take us down beneath our experience to certain animal impulses or physical processes of which our feelings are only an illusory superstructure. Once one knows Aristophanes' speech, it is very difficult to forget it when one most needs it. It is the speech for an experience that is speechless.[8]

—Why do the speechless need a speech? Why is it not enough that each of these lovers finds the other "to his taste"? "To his taste" is more literally translatable as "to his *mind*." Pausanias was more honest here, in his emphasis on the intellect of the beloved, for it is Pausanias and not Aristophanes who presents the lover's perspective from the inside. What applies to Pausanias' speech thus applies also to Aristophanes', that it points beyond itself to Socratic education through conversation or dialogue, ultimately to dialectics.—Then again, perhaps Aristophanes intends his excessively corporeal account of love in part as a comic caricature of Pausanias' speech, which gives an intellectual pretense to an essentially speechless longing for sexual gratification with the young. Perhaps!—In other words, when Aristophanes says that "love is the name for the desire and pursuit of the whole," what does he mean by "the whole"? The whole human being, our ancient nature? Or the whole as such, the whole of things? And do we wish to *rule* the whole of things, as the original, arrogant circle-men? Or rather only to *understand* it, so far as possible? Aristophanes points beyond his speechless lovers to prating politicians and chattering philosophers—he points above all to Socrates. What is he trying to say, though? Socrates is no monster, he has no wish to rule in place of the gods, he will merely deny the divinity of Eros. But what about those who listen to him, what about his retinue of lovers? What will become of them?—

16. Diomedes

"Why," you may wonder, "a section on Diomedes, when he is nowhere mentioned in the *Symposium*?" Nowhere mentioned, yes, but certainly alluded to. Aristophanes remarks, apparently in passing, that what Homer says of Ephialtes and Otos's assault on the Olympian gods is true also of man in his ancient nature. Homer speaks twice of Ephialtes and Otos, once in the *Odyssey*, as Odysseus takes his tour of Hades, and then in the *Iliad*, in Dione's consolation to Aphrodite upon being wounded by Diomedes, the same Diomedes who will immediately go on to wound Ares. Do you see what Aristophanes has done here? He directs us to Homer for a glimpse of our ancient nature, only for us to find that our arrogant ancestors took our *present* form, that the circle-men are not a long-lost kind of man, a monstrous kind of man, but an image for a present possibility, still available to man today. Why else would Aristophanes ever mention Zeus' threat of a second cutting, of further punishment, unless we might do it again in our current state? And what is the desire to depose the gods, to usurp their place, but *erōs*, the same attempt at self-divinization that will soon grip the Athenians? Aristophanes' praise of *erōs* thus hides a subtle narrowing of *erōs* from its vertical or hierarchical form to its horizontal or egalitarian form.—"But," one might object, "Diomedes only succeeds in wounding Ares thanks to Athena's help, that is, thanks to the help of a goddess, so how could he be a present possibility? Aristophanes is then *right* to restrict our *erōs* to love of another person, for only there is its object attainable." It's questionable whether even then it's truly attainable, but that's beside the present point. Yes, only Athena is quick and strong enough to swat away Ares' volley at Diomedes and to drive Diomedes' spear into the god's belly, but it is no less true that on his own Diomedes can indeed head toward Ares and aim. Though the power is divine, the intention is still human. We might be doomed to failure, but didn't Ephialtes and Otos also fail? We learn in the *Odyssey* that they were but children at the time.—"All the same, why the allusion, why not state this outright?" To mention the vertical form of *erōs* would have rendered the horizontal form wholly unattractive. Perhaps this is not true of you, perhaps you find Aristophanes' account on its face most true and satisfying; but it is certainly true of these Athenians, in the grips of *erōs* on the eve of the Sicilian Expedition. Aristophanes praises *erōs* while subtly narrowing its object, that is, while criticizing it *sotto voce*. By this rhetorical strategy, he hopes to achieve his vision of a religious transformation in his home city, as those present spread the gospel to the rest of the Athenians, who will then build new temples and altars and make great sacrifices to this old but woefully underappreciated god, Eros, a god whose blessings they already receive and will continue to receive with every embrace of their other half, up to satiety. Imagine what might have happened, had he succeeded in converting the gathering at Agathon's house, in these precious few months before the Sicilian Expedition, imagine the sight of Alcibiades by the ships alone, hoping to depart for Sicily, as his troops lay at home in the blissful repose of post-coital slumber. What a feat of salvation, and in the eleventh hour of Athens' ill-fated expedition!—"But he fails, he *doesn't* convert the group." Who is this speech for, then? At more than a few points, it's clear from the language used, the language of life-long companionship and even of being welded together, that the sort of lasting relationship Aristophanes envisions would appeal above all to Pausanias. Yet what does it matter if Pausanias is convinced but not his beloved, Agathon? Could Aristophanes really have persuaded *him*? Agathon, who just won the prize for his tragedy, in whose ears still ring the applause of Athens? Whom Aristophanes himself mocked for his libertine sexual practices, and whom Plato depicts at the end of the dialogue on a couch with Socrates and Alcibiades, engaged in a flirtatious game of musical chairs? Would *this* Agathon ever want to give everything up and go home, in the vigor of youth, though not to say the prime of life, to bask in the loving gaze and embrace of Pausanias, his elder lover? Aristophanes is kidding himself, if he thinks such men as Agathon would worship at the altar of domestic *erōs*, of *erōs* domesticated. And not just Agathon, for Athens abounds in such men.—But perhaps Aristophanes knows this all too well, perhaps he really is kidding himself and knows that the joke is on him. He himself admits it would be a joke to think of Pausanias and his beloved Agathon as an example of such lovers. Aristophanes concedes that he has nothing to say to men like Agathon. "Athens is too far gone," he must think, smiling to himself, with more than a hint of sadness. "Pausanias is damned to an empty bed. So much for his 'education' in virtue!" But then where will Agathon be? Who is waiting for him? And to whom will he go?

17. The Ancient Quarrel

It is often remarked that the *Symposium* gives us a live example of what Socrates calls in the *Republic* "the ancient quarrel between poetry and philosophy," that it gives us the *exemplar* of that quarrel. The quarrel concerns who is wisest, and as with any quarrel settling it requires a standard, here a standard of wisdom. But the standard of wisdom is the very thing at issue in whether the poet or the philosopher is wisest, and even then which sort of poet and which sort of philosopher—it is the standard of nature, it concerns what nature is and to what sort of life nature so understood directs us, to the life of the poet or the life of the philosopher. But by focusing on nature, do we not already settle the question in favor of the philosopher?—No, the correct question is rather, Why does settling the question of *erōs* necessarily involve the question of nature?

18. Is Socrates a Lover of Boys?

After Socrates, no one speaks about philosophy as much as Pausanias—not Apollodorus, not Alcibiades, nobody.[9] That alone wouldn't suffice to confuse him with Socrates, for who could ever mistake Aristodemus or Apollodorus for the man himself? But pair that with Pausanias' eyebrow-raising relationship with the youth, along with his emphasis on education and virtue, and you begin to understand the suspicion with which some Athenian fathers may have viewed Socrates' motives, upon learning that their sons, even the noblest, eagerly went to this shoeless smooth-talker for an "education." Plato saves Socrates from this false impression by having him advocate on behalf of a non-corporeal erotic relationship with the youth, on behalf of what has come to be known as Platonic love, all backed up by Alcibiades' unsolicited testimony. But who does Plato save, really? Who stands to benefit by this distinction? Pausanias, whose way of life is plausibly legitimate, according to the standards of Athenian conventions? Or Socrates, whose way of life was found by the same to be a capital crime? And doesn't Socrates actively cultivate this false impression? Doesn't he play at being a Pausanias-type? Take what happens in the *Charmides*, for example. There Socrates tells the story of his conversation with the beautiful, young Charmides, upon whose entrance all were completely enamored, including, it seems, even Socrates himself. But a closer look shows that not Socrates but all the others were in the grips of *erōs* for Charmides, while Socrates rather *wondered* at his beauty, looking not so much at Charmides himself but at how everyone else looked at Charmides. Or take the *Lysis*, where

Socrates gives Hippothales tips on how to win his beautiful beloved, Lysis, effectively offering up his services as a *pro bono* pick-up artist for pederasts. Socrates offers to show Hippothales how it's done and fulfills that offer by convincing Lysis, much to Hippothales' visible excitement, that a beloved must gratify his lover. Yet Socrates immediately shows that their conclusion is open to a host of queries that expose their ignorance, much to the disappointment, we imagine, of Hippothales, who has seen his quarry barely escape his grasp. So, while Socrates actively cultivates the false impression that he has the same interest in the youth as Pausanias, both in the *Symposium* and elsewhere, a closer look shows that his interest is heavily moderated, if not entirely governed, by the distinctively philosophic passion of wonder, a passion that arises not in gazing upon the beautiful beloved but in the face of one's ignorance before basic perplexities. And how much more uncivilized is *this* passion than that of *erōs*?

19. The Tragedy of Aristophanes

I agree with the conclusion many others have drawn about Aristophanes' speech, that it's essentially tragic. Is there really another half somewhere out there, waiting to complete me? And even if there is, how can I know that she, to whom I cleave, truly is that half? And even if she truly is, how could I ever achieve the desired unity? And even if I somehow achieved that unity, even if Hephaestus did come down and actually fulfilled his offer to weld me to her, would I be happy? Would I even *be*? Is that what my love amounts to, a desire to cease to be? Do I really love out of a sense of incompleteness, out of yearning to escape my poor, sad, fragmentary self? And what about her? Does she, in turn, love me for these very same reasons? But how could she love me? How could I love her? How could anyone love a lover, a broken fragment of a being? What, then, do we really love when we "love" another?

Plato puts a tragic account of love in the mouth of a comic poet, of *the* comic poet, Aristophanes, as it very much suits Plato's sense of humor to make a tragic figure of the comic poet.—Let's not discount Aristophanes so quickly, now. Is he so unaware of this joke, of the tragic implications of his speech? He surely tries to make it funny, but the jokes are all superficial, superficial because mere images, likenesses floating on the surface of the tale to conceal its tragic implications. And they conceal those implications by translating the most troubling details into the lowly and ridiculous: the circle-people roll, "just like" tumbling acrobats; they are spherical, "similar" to their planetary parents, and cut in half, "just like" eggs and apples; they generate children in the ground, "just like" cicadas, rather than the male in the female, as now; and we today might still be cut in half again, "just like" dice, so that we would look "just like" stone reliefs. From what do these comic images distract? From our original arrogance, our lost wholeness, and our present incompleteness, from the sad fact that reproduction is a poor palliative against the ills of our present condition, from the suspicion that our original arrogance may not have departed us...—But what of the circle-people themselves? Are they not comic yet presented literally? Or should we not ask of what are they an image? Here's one important possibility. The navel, Aristophanes says, is Apollo's reminder to us of our ancient nature. But does anyone look at his navel and think of being a circle-person? No, or rather not unless the original circle-people are a comic image for our pregnant mothers. But then for what would our longing be?

20. Frogs and Clouds

We cannot praise the beauty of the *Symposium* without also praising that of Aristophanes' *Frogs*, which played no small part in inspiring Plato. In the *Frogs*, Dionysus disguises himself in a lion skin to appear nobler than he is, to appear as his half-brother Heracles, and ventures into Hades to rescue a prize-winning poet, Euripides, for his pleasure; ultimately, however, he undergoes an education that shifts his concern from his pleasure to the salvation of Athens, so he ends up leaving with a different poet, Aeschylus. Similarly, in the *Symposium*, Socrates disguises himself in clean clothing to appear more beautiful than he is and ventures to Agathon's house to rescue a prize-winning poet, Agathon, for...what? And does Socrates also undergo an education? Does he learn? And if so, what? And who is the poet he leaves with, if not Agathon? This, at least, we can answer: Plato.—

21. Numb Tongues and Deaf Ears

Aristophanes began speaking by hoping out loud that those present would spread his speech far and wide. Judged by that hope, Aristophanes' speech is a manifest failure. Why does Aristophanes fail? More pointedly: Socrates praises Eryximachus' speech and anticipates Agathon will speak well. He is silent about Aristophanes. Why doesn't Socrates praise Aristophanes' speech? Why the quiet but clear disapproval?—Let's start here: Aristophanes' tongue-tied lovers don't know what they want, yet each somehow selects that beloved which is "to his taste," literally, "to his *mind* (*nous*)." Just after Aristophanes finishes, Agathon prefaces his speech by observing that he is not "ignorant that to a man who has mind (*nous*) a few who are thoughtful (*emphrones*) are more terrifying than many who are thoughtless (*aphrones*)." How else could minds meet but through speech? But what is the interplay of fear and love in the meeting of minds through conversation? The answer can be found in what Socrates attempts to do with Agathon, but more vividly in what he already did many years before with Alcibiades—it can be found, that is, in Alcibiades' exposure of Socrates' love-games and confession of humiliation at his hands. Were Alcibiades not drunk, he'd have been as silent as Aristophanes' lovers before Hephaestus.

22. Socrates' First Dialogue with Agathon

As the group turns from Aristophanes to Agathon, Socrates takes the mere mention of his name as an invitation to engage Agathon in conversation; the young poet happily obliges in what appears to be witty banter, picking up on their earlier dialogue, during dinner, about Agathon's concern with popular praise. Agathon claims to have greater shame before the intelligent few than the unintelligent many. Whereas Socrates fears the many, and so praises Agathon's courage, Agathon claims to fear these sensible few, presumably those present—though as we soon see, his speech is so successful, wins such universal applause, that his confession of fear seems to be an ironic courtesy more than anything else. But Socrates' primary concern is not whether Agathon would feel shame before the wise but whether he'd ever do anything shameful before the many. Or how does Socrates mean *ti aischron poiein*? "To do something shameful"? Or "to make something ugly"? Is he asking if Agathon would be willing to make poems, to write books, that the many think ugly but the few deem beautiful? And not even those few present, but some unknown few whom Socrates says Agathon might eventually meet, the unknown wise who might encounter the "ugly" thing Agathon has made? Is he willing, in other words, to do what Plato allegedly did, would he burn his tragedies upon meeting Socrates and write instead philosophic dialogues, Socratic dialogues? But he already knows Socrates, and he has yet to burn his tragedies, far from it.—So then what is Socrates after with this poet? What need does a philosopher old and ugly have for a poet young and beautiful, a poet like Agathon?

23. Agathon's Speech

There's a cheekiness to Agathon's impiety, to his ironic genuflection about the sacred law and divine indignation, since he more or less admits that no one present believes in the gods, that even the greatest poets may have lied about them. Nobody takes his pious overtures seriously, as genuine piety, rather all discern Agathon's wink and nod to those gathered at his home, all notice the playfulness—to use Agathon's term—of his speech, which he so designs as to display the manipulative power that poetry has put at his disposal. Agathon's praise of Eros is, as all readily recognize, ultimately a praise of Agathon himself: not Eros, but Agathon is the young, tender poet, supple in his accommodation of others and well-proportioned in his looks, and above all capable, in his wisdom, of creating friendship and peace both among his guests and beyond. His speech is a masterpiece of urbane and enlightened wit, *le plat principal de ce banquet.*

Supple indeed! Agathon's winks to the few over the heads of the many do more, much more than give the lie to his pious overtures; they rather suggest to them his special insight into the nature of things. In his barely concealed self-praise of "Eros" as the wise poet, our prize-winning host identifies his art as the cause of everything beautiful and good, an assertion of right that makes sense only if a world without poetry is ugly and harsh, only if the poet hides the deadly truth about our violent natural state. Agathon therefore claims that, prior to Eros' reign, Necessity was queen, under whose dominion occurred the fabled castrations and bindings of the gods. All gratitude is therefore owed, it would seem, to the poet Eros, whose ascendance to the throne has at long last brought the world to a state of peace. Yet Agathon also suggests that Eros' predecessor under the reign of Necessity, the age of which the ancient poets like Hesiod and Homer sung, was Ate, Deception—or, rather, that Eros *is* Ate, that Love *is* Deception. Does Eros even rule? Or do his pacifying poems belong rather to Ate, who deceives us into believing that Necessity's reign is at an end? Is Eros just a male pseudonym for this wily goddess? The poet, Agathon confirms via wink, can only be the cause of friendship and peace, his achievement can only be noteworthy, against the backdrop of a harsh nature; the poet can rescue man from reality, but only if his poetry deceives man, only if without the poet's deceptions the life of man would be solitary, poor, nasty, brutish, and short. Agathon thus brings the deeply nihilistic, sophistic view into the arena of these speeches, a view no doubt to the taste of those enlightened few gathered at his home, those same few we also find gathered in the sophistic *milieu* of the *Protagoras*—save, of course, Aristophanes.

Agathon thus cons the many and delights the few, while articulating mythically and thus implicitly man's place in the cosmos. It's here that we may sense him speaking primarily to Socrates, explaining his interest in him by suggesting that both men, poet and philosopher, share a peculiar sort of moderation, based not in moral self-restraint—a vulgar sort of moderation—but in a single desire's domination to the exclusion of all others. Yet despite this similarity, Agathon also identifies an essential difference between them, one that redounds to the credit of the poet, whose ability to accommodate others frees him of the fear that so bothered the unaccommodating philosopher, the simply rude Socrates. Agathon thus answers Socrates' question: he needn't choose between making something beautiful to the many or something beautiful to the few, for he can do both at once, becoming thereby the cause of the great peace they all enjoy. If Eros is Agathon, in his youthful tenderness and accommodating suppleness, in his seemly proportions, then what is the old, hard-skulled baldy, the rude and ugly Socrates, but the exemplar of anti-eroticism?—"You call *this* accommodating? Agathon's speech is far ruder than anything Socrates has done or said!" But what could please Socrates more than this, a witty and ironic *riposte* in their dialogue, hidden in a speech that speaks to all levels of humanity at once?—Anti-erotic indeed: Socrates confessed his fear of the many, he therefore praised Agathon's courage, but his courage, Agathon informs us, is akin to Eros' defeat of Ares, *à la* Diomedes; it lies in his establishing peace among all warring parties, and that feat he accomplishes through what Socrates no less than Agathon attributes to Eros: he accomplishes it through *poetry*. Socrates' fear is just the obverse of his lack of *erōs*, without which they would not be enjoying the present peace.—The present peace the work of *erōs*? It was the work of a wholly unerotic man, Nicias! Not the peace but the looming expedition to Sicily proved to be the peak expression of Athens' erotic yearning for superhuman wholeness. And in any case, since when has love ever been the cause of peace?[10]

24. Deafening Applause

Why does Agathon win such universal praise? Properly understood, his speech answers the thrust of Socrates' line of questioning, abruptly cut off by Phaedrus, who insists that Agathon fulfill his obligation; yet it also fulfills that obligation by offering a speech in praise of Eros; it therefore meets the general challenge, a contest of speeches, winning universal applause from all present; and it likewise speaks with the requisite yet ironic pious overtures, so that the speech would, if it ever got out to the many, as indeed it does, appear all mercy, all faith, all honesty, all humanity, all religion. The youthful poet Agathon is truly supple in his looks, able to shift shapes according to the inclinations and intelligence of his audience, earning him rightly the universal applause he receives. It makes sense why all those present applaud, seeing that almost all of them are products of the sophistic "Enlightenment," as evidenced by their presence in the *Protagoras*—all, that is, save Aristophanes and Aristodemus. Xenophon answers well enough about Aristodemus.[11] But what about Aristophanes? Did he really applaud? How could he, when Agathon's speech confirms his judgment that Agathon is symptomatic of the illness that plagues Athens? Or did Aristodemus, who reports the gathering's universal approval, simply not notice Aristophanes' reaction? Aristophanes, we recall, appeared to have urged the gathering to pass over Aristodemus, skipping him to get to Agathon, only for Agathon now to succeed where Aristophanes had failed, in winning over those gathered. So did Aristodemus delight in seeing Aristophanes get his comeuppance? But if, again, Agathon's speech inadvertently confirms Aristophanes' diagnosis, then the success of Agathon's speech is a credit to Aristophanes' wisdom. If anything, it's *Socrates'* wisdom that Agathon discredits. Was Aristodemus so eager to see Aristophanes get his due that he didn't notice what Agathon had implied about Aristodemus' beloved Socrates?—But why does any of this even matter? Why even give such care and attention to such a small and forgettable man as Aristodemus?

25. The Six Speeches

There are six speeches in praise of *erōs*. How do they fit together? Strauss divides them into uninspired and inspired speeches. The first three are uninspired, in that each subordinates *erōs* to something outside it, while the latter three are inspired, in that each analyzes *erōs* according to its own, inherent ends.—But then why even have the first three? Why not skip straight to the more direct, immanent analysis of *erōs*? Because the first three sketch the typical restraints on our erotic rebellion. Phaedrus subordinates *erōs* to gain, material gain. There's love, yes, but there's also marriage, and one really ought to marry sensibly (for money, and preferably to a doctor). Pausanias, too, subordinates *erōs* to something external, morality, and his whole speech is a caricature of the sweaty-palmed, moral self-restraint of the longing for the beauty of youth. And Eryximachus? He subordinates *erōs* to art, to *technē*, that is, to rational-technical manipulation of nature for the sake of balance and harmony.—But if Plato's concern is the unbridled *erōs* of the Sicilian Expedition, and these are the typical restraints, why include the latter three speeches, those of the poets Aristophanes and Agathon and the philosopher Socrates? Or is this not already clear? These Athenians are on the eve of the Sicilian Expedition, their erotic venture *par excellence*, so the conventional restraints no longer work; if a restraint is to be found, it must come from within, it must be intrinsic to *erōs* itself. After Eryximachus, *erōs* is essentially rebellious. Aristophanes reveals it. Agathon exemplifies it. And Socrates? He cures it—

26. The Challenge Before Socrates

But what is the challenge the poets level before the philosopher in their quarrel? Aristophanes sensed the threat *erōs* posed to imperial Athens, that the city yearned for redemption and ultimately transcendence, that such ambition risked, in its attempt at superhuman wholeness, collapsing under its own, hubristic weight. Aristophanes' "solution" was to conceal a restraint of *erōs* beneath a praise of *erōs*, of a private and domestic form of *erōs*, love of another as one's missing half, on pains of divine punishment. Piety domesticates love. Aristophanes ultimately conceded, however, that his speech is likely too little too late: though he can speak to Pausanias, he cannot speak to Pausanias' beloved, Agathon. For the very same Agathon, whom Aristophanes threatens with divine vengeance for further assault on the gods, rejects them entirely in outright atheism, which not only declares his disbelief in them but pronounces the poet's arrogant pride as their *maker*. Is Agathon the circle-man in human form? He combines the goddess Ate and the god Eros into an androgynous alternative to the Olympian gods, but more fundamentally he argues that the seductive femininity of his poetry is identical to courage or manliness. The connection is more than speculative, by the way, for the androgyn of Aristophanes' speech appears to be a reference to his play, the *Thesmophoriazousai*, in which he credits Agathon for his flexibility, adaptability, or accommodation, while also mocking him for his androgyny, that is, for wearing feminine clothing, shaving his body of all hair, and "being ridden like a horse." (*Now* we see what Agathon *really* learned from Pausanias!) This combination or androgyny is, no doubt, a symptom of the psychic illness plaguing Athens, to which illness Aristophanes admits he has no remedy. It is Agathon, then, who becomes the locus for the quarrel between poetry and philosophy. After Aristophanes speaks, Socrates praises Eryximachus and anticipates that Agathon will speak well. His silence about Aristophanes is his quiet way of signaling his disapproval, of suggesting that more can be done for Athens, that there is another path to restraining Athens' *erōs*.—But let's not confuse things: this is no mere political dispute. For the political dispute concerns the means for restraining *erōs*, it thus turns on the question of the nature of *erōs*, and settling the question of *erōs* promises, we have suggested, to settle the question of nature.

27. Eros, Damned with False Praise

The friendship established by Agathon's speech doesn't last long, nor could it, since his universal accommodation required paying Socrates' prodding questions and insinuations back with a barb of his own, and Socrates rarely lets such mischaracterizations go unanswered.[12] He doesn't just point the finger at Agathon, however, but at the whole group—Does he include Aristodemus?—for praising love not with an eye to the truth but with an eye to the ignorance, or passivity, of their audience. Agathon's impressive and genial accommodation of the many and the few, and of the few and the one, ultimately fails: he can satisfy Phaedrus only by disappointing Socrates. And so the long-simmering tension between Socrates and the other Athenians finally boils over into outright hostility, as Socrates issues his accusation and presents the truth of praising anything, love included.

True praise, Socrates claims, involves telling the *truth*. But because what one praises may not be praiseworthy as whole, may not be wholly beautiful or noble, one must first select the most beautiful truths, omitting all else, and then arrange them in as conspicuously attractive a manner as possible. What are Socrates' misleading omissions? How has he arranged his speech deceptively? That is, what must we add to his speech, and how must we rearrange its parts? To wit: What are the proper parts of *erōs*, and what their proper order? Only by answering these questions, Socrates intimates, will we know what love is. Anything short of that risks mistaking a partial truth for the whole truth, of mistaking a poetic whole for the true whole. Socrates plays the poet.

—"If Socrates omits whatever is not 'most beautiful' about love, then clearly his *full* account must be exceedingly sober and cynical." Sobering, yes, but cynical? Not necessarily. Will his sobering critique of love really be much worse than anything we've already heard? Haven't the others, in uttering falsehoods about Love, damned him with false praise? And have they not, in so doing, failed to state the beautiful truths that Socrates will go on to share? Socrates' complete account of love may be more sober, less sexy than those before him, but it will for that very reason also offer truer guidance as to the place of love in a human life, and of that life in the whole.—But we should never forget that, when Alcibiades enters, he will note the innocence and credulity of anyone who'd believe that Socrates actually praised *love*.

28. Socrates' Second Dialogue with Agathon

After some preliminary questions, Socrates engages Agathon in a line of questioning that exposes his ignorance about *erōs*, that compels the poet to confess openly his ignorance himself, that therefore repays Agathon's mockery of Socrates by making him look still more ridiculous before his guests than Agathon had Socrates. Anything that loves, Love included, loves and desires only what he does not have, Socrates argues, only what he is in need of, with any apparent desire for what one already possesses merely oriented toward the future, toward the continued and secure possession of the beautiful and good things, on and on and—For how long? Unclear. Relevant, though, is Agathon's failure to object about those things one might still desire despite possessing them, such open-ended desires as one might have for strength, speed, and wealth, ends Socrates presents as concrete, *finite* goods. What is the "something" at which these open-ended, apparently limitless desires aim?—Anyway, Agathon ultimately concedes that Love is *not* beautiful, since it is *of* beauty, he thereby concedes that he spoke ignorantly, an admission on his part that must have embarrassed this host before his guests, which may even have embarrassed the guests themselves, for feting his ignorance. Aristodemus, at least, certainly senses the significance of Agathon's concession. Socrates then produces the same outcome, but for the good things, and now Agathon's agitation becomes visible, as he blames Socrates for the conclusion rather than accepting responsibility himself and, ultimately, admitting the truth.—"What's Socrates doing? What purpose could this serve but to gratify his indignation and resentment at Agathon's insult? What vengeful malice in the knife's thrusts of the syllogism!" But how else was Socrates to proceed? How else could he break the spell of Agathon's success, not just from the day before with his tragedy but even from just now, from the gathering's universal approval of his praise of Love? Shame before his peers is the exact antidote to Agathon's sickness, an inclination to accommodating rhetoric at the price of the truth, to singing lies like the truth to please his audience. The problem? His audience—*this* audience—can also follow an argument, or at least buy into it, especially one as simple as this. Socrates shows Agathon the superiority of dialectic to rhetoric and poetry, not just for discerning truth but for persuading an audience—an audience of his peers, at least. Accommodating the few, Agathon now learns, requires appropriating Socratic dialectic. His shame is salutary. He may even have blushed—Agathon, of all people! At any rate, Socrates has made his point: Agathon must choose an audience. For what hope can Agathon have to please Socrates and the many at once, when he cannot even please Socrates and the few? But to please Socrates, wouldn't Agathon have to settle for a wisdom that is disputable like a dream? Again, what sort of works is he willing to write? What is he willing to make? Does he need the praise of his contemporary Athenians, or will he settle for objections and footnotes?...No? Not even for millennia of them?

29. Why the Young Socrates?

Agathon finds himself in something of a crisis. He is no doubt proud of his poetic victory the day before and the apparent wisdom that engendered it, that it in turn evinced. But he also saved the seat next to him just for Socrates, that ugly oddball, and urged his servants to keep watch for him, only to gently shoo Aristodemus away to sit beside Eryximachus. Then there's all the flirty banter and erotic jousting. And now Socrates betrays his otherwise victorious lover by exposing his ignorance publicly, so that Agathon recoils in shame, only for Socrates to soften the blow by claiming that he, as a young man, said nearly the same things as Agathon. Nearly, but not totally: Socrates is far more willing—too willing, really—to reject Eros, to reject, too, its typical object, the beautiful. A difference of disposition, and no small one, at that. To the point, though, Socrates does the same in the *Phaedo*: he offers an "autobiography" to instruct his audience, at once deeply attracted to his speeches but somewhat deterred by his deeds, that is, to teach them how to be more like him. And in both he attempts, though how successfully is unclear, to turn these lovers of Socrates' "wisdom" into lovers of wisdom simply, or to begin to turn them. This he can do, however, only by distorting philosophy so that it might meet his lovers' demands. *His* development is to become *their* development. Here, then, Agathon sits at the feet of Socrates, much as Socrates purports he had at the feet of Diotima, a Mantinean prophetess. Like Agathon, Socrates exalts the feminine in this gathering of men, and not just with his teacher, Diotima, but with her teaching, which holds that both men and woman are pregnant and bear children; there, philosophy emerges as the highest androgyny, a combination of manly ambition with feminine birthing that cannot but charm Agathon, the poet who seeks with tender verses to pacify the warlike into placidity. How could this fail to attract the cross-dressing Agathon? Diotima is just Socrates in drag.

30. Eros Naturalized

Though every speaker has, to different degrees of explicitness and self-awareness, spoken of Eros both as a god and as a human passion, and for the most part as the latter, Diotima is the first to *transform* Eros from one to the other; she is the first, in other words, to turn Eros into *erōs*, from a god into a natural phenomenon. Eros *cannot* be a god, she argues, for his neediness and lack of the beautiful and good things forbid him the happiness that all gods necessarily, by their very essence, enjoy. But she goes further in her naturalization. Initially, *erōs* is a lesser divinity between gods and men, so that priests and diviners are the exemplary erotics. But by the end, *erōs* is between "the thing that loves" and "the beloved thing," that is, between two abstract neuter nouns—two principles?—so that not the priest or diviner but the philosopher and dialectician is the erotic *par excellence*. What happened?—First, another strange shift. Initially the state between wisdom and ignorance is that of having a correct opinion without being able to give an account of *why* it's correct. Of course, there's no search for the account, for the why, since initially the erotic art is, again, divination or prophecy. One listens to what one is told to do, one *obeys* the correct opinions of the priests, who in turn listen to and obey the gods. But by the end the state between wisdom and ignorance is rather philosophy, the active search for the truth out of a sense of one's resourcelessness, a *resourceful* resourcelessness. Diotima thus starts from orthodoxy and pious obedience to priests and prophets, on the one hand, and shifts to philosophy, the perplexed search for the abstract truth through reason and reason alone, on the other.—So what happened?

Where have the gods gone? Where the priests and diviners? On what basis have they been excluded, banned, cast out? Or did they leave of their own accord? Why is pious obedience to the gods inadequate as an understanding of *erōs*? What's the argument? Or have the priests become philosophers, interpreters of the divine's ordering of things? So much turns on this: replacing the gods with "the beloved thing" paves the way for the object of *erōs* to become the wholly abstract "the beautiful itself" at the peak of Diotima's speech. The argument has been omitted, and didn't Socrates say he would omit from his speech only what is not beautiful?—But how do we find an omission, what is missing? We have to look at the text, at the passage right there before us, and find the problem inherent therein, and only therein. What happens there?

31. Poverty and Plenty

"Who is Eros' father," the young Socrates asks, "and mother?" Diotima responds with a memorable tale of the "courtship" of Eros' parents and his conception. Eros' father is Poros, whose name variously means Plenty, Resource, or even Way, while his mother is Penia or Poverty. The occasion for their *rendez-vous*, and Eros' conception, was the birth of Aphrodite—take a look at Hesiod's version of the tale, by the way, and think of the Herms—in whose celebration there was a dinner and even drinking, though in this pre-oenological era it was nectar they imbibed. Among the drunk was Poros, who eventually wandered away from the gathering into the garden of Zeus, and there fell asleep, presumably uncovered and on the ground. Penia, who had come begging, was apparently denied entry, but there saw Poros sleeping, and so plotted, on account of her own lack of resources, to make a child from Poros, from Resource, reclining beside him in the garden and thus conceiving her boy. Diotima then translates her myth into something of an account, and here, when she explains how Eros resembles his father, how his mother, the matter gets hopelessly confused. For while Love does indeed resemble Poverty, in his neediness, and Plenty, in his resourcefulness, Diotima attributes the lover's plotting to his father, though it was Penia who plotted, and the lover's sleeping outside uncovered to his mother, though that was Poros. We could chalk this confusion up, of course, to the difficulty of giving a genetic account of *erōs*, that is, an account of Eros the divinity in terms of his conception, since *erōs* the passion would already have to exist, one hopes, for Eros to be conceived. But there's more to it than that, since Love proves resource*ful* most of all, Diotima says, in his plotting for beautiful things and for good things, yet the plotting of Poverty was rooted rather in her *lack* of resources, or of Resource (*dia tēn hautēs aporian*). Love—rather, lovers seem more impoverished than resourceful; they are nevertheless resourceful, of course, though not because they already possess their beloved, but because they come well-equipped with tricks, because they ably weave their schemes. Poros had to get drunk and sleep outside for Penia to trap him, the goal had to be lowered—somewhat lowered, though not *too* much—from the banquet of the gods to the grove outside, and from voluntary coupling to drunken fornication or, to be frank, to the outright rape, or at least near rape, of Poros—"Of what is *that* an allegory? What corresponds to *that* part of the myth?" A difficult question, but here's a start. According to Diotima, the lover's resourcelessness leads him to plot for beautiful and good things, it engenders thereby tricks and schemes, and so he becomes a sophist or philosopher. To answer this question, then, we must first come to know how successful these plots are, could ever be, whether they attain the beautiful and good, and *kalokagathia* is in some sense or other possible; we must, in other words, examine the ends of *erōs* and their relationship to one another, and not just in isolation, as Aristophanes and Agathon had done with love of one's own and love of the beautiful, but also together and in light of the most obviously rational and lovable or desirable end, the good—rather, good things. "Since this is the sort of thing love is," the young Socrates next asks, "what use does he have for human beings?" He sees what love is after, what it wants, and he accepts, at least for now, that *erōs* is the philosophic passion, but now, in asking whether *erōs* has any use for us, he effectively asks, Does *erōs* ever actually deliver? Does it ever attain its object? Is philosophic consummation even possible? If so, how? And with what?

32. The Dance

When young Socrates asks, "What use does love have for human beings?," he challenges Diotima, compels her, to give reasons, *good* reasons, for pursuing the object of our *erōs*. She begins from the beautiful things, and young Socrates readily agrees that the love of beautiful things includes the love that they be one's own, a desire for possession. But when asked what will be for him, who possesses the beautiful things, he cannot answer. Why? What's the meaning of Socrates' silence here? Does he not see the worthiness of possessing beautiful things? Or are beautiful things manifestly self-justifying, that is, do they need no further rationale in the mind of their pursuer? Which applies to Socrates, the young Socrates? He answers more readily regarding the good things, as he knows that he who loves the good things loves that they become his, and that he who possesses them will be happy. Would young Socrates be happy, then, with a good life lacking in beauty? But let's be careful here: though the argument is straightforward, it contains caveats and unstated, certainly unexplored, possibilities. The good things certainly *promise* happiness, but do the beautiful things not do the same? The promise of the good things is more *explicit*; the beautiful things, however, in being self-justifying in the eyes of their lovers, need no further justification, no further *reason*, whether good or bad, lest they be judged before some higher standard and thus no longer be an end in themselves—the promise is therefore *implicit*, and it is a promise the lover deems already kept in the very act of possession, in holding and beholding. The beautiful things present themselves as an end in themselves, but they seem now to young

Socrates a dead end. He seems now to require good reasons to continue further down that path. "But what about the promise of the good things, is it any less of a promise, even if more explicit, even if calling therefore for justification, for *good* reasons? 'Your answer,' Diotima says, '*seems* to be complete.'" But if the good things don't keep this promise, if the good things, to be good, must be possible, and the best life possible for you isn't a happy one, then can such a life really be an object of *erōs*? Is such a life really so appealing that it could ever arouse a passion that yearns for transformation and transcendence? Everyone *wants* the good, to live a happy life, but do they really do all those ridiculous things lovers do? Diotima is aware of the difficulty. Young Socrates' responses, his resistance to the beautiful things as a path to happiness, force her on a digression, to re-route her argument through the good things. Through a bit of sophistry, certainly not her last, she presents the situation with *erōs*, the word, as analogous to that with the word *poiēsis*, which generally means "making" of any kind but most conspicuously means the making of the poet, "poetry." Likewise, *erōs* generally means love of the good things but most conspicuously refers to the all-consuming love of the beautiful beloved. And through another bit of sophistry—I told you it wasn't her last!—she associates our desire *always* to have the good things, *always* to live good lives, as a desire to live good lives *always* and thus to live *forever*. And this is to say nothing about the biggest sophistry, yet to come, the one that earns her the title of a *perfect* sophist.—All this at the right time and in the proper place. But where Diotima and the young Socrates most align is on her retreat from the beautiful things to the good things, prior to her subsequent advance, in her final lesson to young Socrates, back toward the beautiful things, and ultimately toward the beautiful itself, where her argument is again met with a chilly reception. Young Socrates forces her to begin from the good things, to establish them as the court before which all the other ends of *erōs*—indeed, all ends simply—are to be judged. That includes the beautiful, Agathon's end. But it also includes one's own, the end Aristophanes proposed. And the judgment against one's own that Diotima offers, and young Socrates confirms, is severe: better to excise one's own, if it is bad; if anything is one's own, it is *the good as such*. (Socrates here seems to break the fourth wall almost entirely.)[13] A strange dance is going on here, as Socrates and Diotima ally against Aristophanes as critics of the love of one's own, Socrates and Aristophanes against Diotima and Agathon as critics of love of the beautiful, Agathon and Aristophanes against Socrates and Diotima as defenders of the gods (however ironically), and Socrates, Diotima, and Aristophanes against Agathon as defenders of limited *erōs*, or *erōs* as limited by nature. It is in this dance, a dance *dramatico-dialecticus*, that the question of *erōs* is settled. So, too, the question of nature—

33. The Love of Nothing

And let's not forget that the first thing Socrates asks Agathon is whether Love is of something or of nothing. Agathon readily affirms that Love is Love of something. Socrates is famous for asking *what* this or that thing is, yet he is less famous for the sort of question he poses here, *whether* this or that thing is something at all—strange, too, since he asks it quite often, and since it's manifestly more fundamental than his more famous "what-is" question. For prior to learning *what* (*ti*) this or that is, you need to know that it's *something* (*ti*). Yet as often as Socrates asks it, neither he nor his interlocutor ever offers an argument to show that it is indeed something; rather, that it is something is always only agreed and therefore assumed. And if the assumption is wrong? What's the status of the conversation that follows? To try to define "something" that is actually nothing is to attempt to situate a non-being among the beings. Where could it go? How could the beings ever accommodate it? Such an accommodation would be forced, the pressure would inevitably expose the "something" for a homeless phantom, behind which hides *nothing.*[14] But returning to the *Symposium*—what *is* Love of?

34. Diotima's Lesson(s)

Socrates' speech relates a lesson he apparently learned from Diotima. But the speech consists rather of two parts, each of which begins and ends *in media res*, so that essential context is omitted: what initiated the conversations and what their outcome was. The first part begins with Socrates advocating nearly the same position as Agathon, but only *nearly*. How did the young Socrates' position differ? Surely he didn't, like Agathon, give a grand speech in praise of the poet as the exemplary erotic at a gathering in his honor. And he's certainly more receptive, too receptive even, of the argument against *erōs* as beautiful and good. The first part ends with young Socrates' chilly reception of Diotima's attempt to connect love of the good to reproduction in the beautiful. She briefly tries to support her point, only for the narration to cut off. What did Socrates respond? Did he even respond at all? If not, why not? The beginning of the second part suggests that the conversation that preceded it in some ways resembled the first part, in others not. Apparently, Diotima repeated the first part a few times, or perhaps the older Socrates composed it out of a few separate lessons, weaving them together poetically into one. What does the older Socrates omit? And from where? From the first part or the second? Both? At the end of the second part, Diotima poses three questions, none of which receives an answer from the young Socrates—nor from the older Socrates. This silence is apparently in keeping with the young Socrates' generally more passive demeanor, as he sits audience to Diotima's exposition of the role of the beautiful in mortal man's attempt to approximate, to the degree possible, the gods' immortality through glory or fame. Why does the young Socrates sit audience to Diotima's exposition? Is he indifferent, disinterested, unimpressed? Or has Diotima so convinced him of every word she says that he sits in silent agreement, even obedience, to her exposition? But how can that be, when at the end of the first part he resisted the basic premise of this exposition, that the love of the good necessarily leads to reproduction? Has the mature Socrates made a conversation rife with objections and disagreements more seemly, has he polished it by omitting how they begin and, more importantly, how they end? And how they fit together, what their proper order is, not the order in time so much as the order in being?—However we choose to resolve these problems, we cannot but admit that resolving them requires some speculation about what happened in the bits of dialogue omitted from these lessons. We ask, again: What are Socrates' omissions, and how are we to order his speech?

35. "Always"

Diotima ultimately concludes that *erōs* is of the good's being one's own always, and to young Socrates' emphatic approval. Yet when she attempts to establish a connection between *erōs* and a concern for immortality, young Socrates resists. Apparently, he does not take "always" to mean "forever" or "for all of time" but "all the time" or "for one's whole life."[15] Young Socrates' *erōs* is peculiar, then, in its aversion to reproduction, to the attempt to overcome the natural limit of one's life. He resists the charm of "the one departing and aged leaving another young one behind, such as he was." Such as he was: this child is at best an imperfect image of oneself, and even if he were a perfect image, he would still only be "such as" you were, he would still be an image and not *you*. This is no immortality, but a wispy, flimsy, weak consolation against death. But at what cost? For this you give up on the more modest aim—modest because possible and simply human—the less sexy or un-sexy, though not to say unambitious and easy aim of the good's being one's own "all the time" or "one's whole life." No, you abandon the concrete and finite goods available within a mortal life for an open-ended or limitless desire. You abandon thereby *living well.*

36. The Perfect Sophist

We've already picked apart some of Diotima's sophisms, but more remain, not least the exaggerated discontinuity in ourselves, for without such discontinuity, how attractive could reproduction be? But let's cut to the chase: Why does Socrates compare Diotima to "the perfect sophists"? And why does he do it when he does?—"'Sophist' is a little strong, is it not? Why not 'expert'?" But she's guilty of obvious sophistry, so why soften the blow? At least observe the sophism.—Diotima here, in this brief segment of the argument, attempts to connect sexual reproduction to the quest for fame by presenting both as paths to immortality rooted in a concern with *honor*. Reproduction gives us a share of immortality—slim as that share may be, and dreadfully slim it is, but that's another story—when "the one departing and old leaves another new one behind, *such as he was*." Such as he was: you lie there, on your deathbed, family gathered bedside, children close beside you, and you look on their faces, so much like your own, you hear their voices, so much like your own, so much of what those voices say reminds you of yourself, of all you learned for yourself and then taught them—you bore them, raised them, educated them, you *formed* them, so far as was in your power, to be like you, *just* like you, so that in some way you will continue to live. All the more so, if they keep and use the stuff you left them! Yes, dreadfully slim, so of course Diotima calls it a device, a trick—But I digress: she draws the crucial, and crucially *broad*, conclusion that "everyone, everything, honors by nature its own offshoot" (a term usually reserved for plants, mind you). It's the next step that leads Socrates to call her a perfect sophist. Asking Socrates to glance, if he wishes, at the love of honor found among human beings, she advances an *equally* broad claim: "everyone does, or makes, everything for immortal virtue and such famous reputation." She thereby identifies, as two offspring of the same source, the father's honoring of his child and the love of honor to be found in those seeking immortality through fame and glory, those poets like Homer or founders like Lycurgus. So, where's the sophistry? Do you see it? Is the love of honor one and the same in both? What does a father honor in his child but himself, the small part of himself that he sees in her? He loves being honored, but by whom? Himself, surely. And the renowned poet or revered lawgiver? He too is the object of honor—not the pale fragment of him, though, as with the father, but he himself. Is he not, therefore, the child? And who are the parents, save those who honor them, the many Greeks who praise Homer for his poetry or the many Spartans who cower in reverent fear before Lycurgus' laws?—"But Homer made them Greeks, Lycurgus made them Spartans. They are the children, those of great men." Yes, they formed these peoples, though not *ex nihilo*, for no matter is so flexible as to enable one to introduce any form you please, not even wax. And might not the reverse be true of the parent, that he must change who he is, if his children are to resemble him, that *he* must accommodate *them*? What parent hasn't had to change his opinion about the good, so that he could continue to love his child? Concede so much, and the sophism becomes plain.—Accept the sophism as gospel, and you no longer see how the love of glory and fame does not preserve you but erases you, makes you disappear as you accommodate those who would honor you, as you meet the terms and conditions in making yourselves beloved to them, much as Phaedrus had described. The lover of honor seeks a life after his life but gains only a death before his death. And the greatest glory goes to the greatest of self-negations, negation however not at the hands of one's offspring but at the hands of the truth, indifferent as it is to its seekers, impersonal as it is in its character. Then philosophy wouldn't be erotic reproduction but rather a morbid longing, so that the *erōs* for wisdom would be a sort of dying and even death. Diotima's sophistry presents self-negation as self-affirmation, and not just any self-affirmation, but the highest possible, the attainment of a personal immortality. It is, indeed, a perfect sophism.—"But for whom? Surely not for Socrates, since he's not been too keen on reproduction." Yes, for whom?

37. The Ladder of Love

In Diotima's mouth, the ladder of beauties she charts are a promise to young Socrates of a grand erotic ascent from the most elementary and immediate experience of beauty, in the beautiful body of the beloved, up to a philosophic vision of perfect beauty, the beautiful itself, proceeding through an ever-increasing awareness of the dependency of the lesser beauties on higher, more expansive or abstract ones. In Socrates' mouth, however, it does more. So much of this ladder speaks to the other symposiasts, not as a negation or refutation of their speeches, but as a challenge to their respective self-understandings, as a re-visioning of each speech and therefore a re-interpretation of each speaker's *erōs*, the speeches being the personal confessions of their authors and a kind of involuntary and unconscious *mémoires*. Socrates integrates each of the symposiasts into a larger whole, giving thereby a shared order and purpose to their lives, culminating finally in a singular aspiration, *philosophy*. For nearly every reference, every image and example in the speech, save Codrus, Lycurgus and Solon—What are they doing there, exactly, Codrus especially?—draws on one of the speeches we've read. We need only trace them back and assemble them in order:

Aristophanes we move past quickly, of course, since Diotima long ago redirected *erōs* away from one's own and toward the good, toward what is truly one's own, which she now attempts to assimilate to the beautiful.

Phaedrus, however, understood the beloved to be higher than the lover, his sacrifices thereby nobler and more deserving of divine rewards. But Socrates now reveals to him that Achilles was also a lover, that he like Alcestis loved immortal fame, so that Phaedrus might find in their lives and in the ladder the source of his own lovability, a beauty that admits of greater expansion than he had hitherto imagined. Socrates widens the eyes of this mercenary beloved. He was, after all, ripe for it: he did attempt, in the end, to show the beloved to be *nobler* than the lover.

Pausanias, too, might find greater structure to his life, as his uneasy mixture of pederasty and morality is directed upward toward the highest study, a philosophic science whose object is the beautiful itself, which in turn promises to make Pausanias all-the-more appealing to his beloveds—all the more respectable, too, to his suspicious fellow citizens, thanks to the anticipated unimpugnable nobility.

Jumping to Eryximachus—he no doubt sees in the physiological imagery a high place for his art of medicine, which might venture beyond its present limitation to corporeal things and develop into a philosophic obstetrics. This newly envisioned art of medicine would include music, and therewith poetry, as Eryximachus had indeed hoped, with the crown and core of the productive arts being that philosophic science of the beautiful.

And finally, Agathon. The freshly feted, prize-winning tragedian, flying high from the day before, though a bit hungover now and thus slowly but surely coming back down from the heavens, to the city and his household: he is offered a new path, an enchanting path, which promises to combine the renown of Homer with the wisdom of Socrates. He need only do for Socrates poetically what Alcibiades attempts politically—appropriate and popularize his wisdom, so far as possible.

But can philosophy really fulfill all these promises? Would Pausanias still maintain his orientation toward the beloved, or would he not eventually be forced to turn away from him and instead look upon the peak of the ladder as the beloved *par excellence*? Would Eryximachus' theoretical discoveries find themselves so adaptable to the technical manipulation of the world, or would he rather have to choose between the productive arts and the wholly contemplative activity of philosophy? Let's not forget, too, the question of *what* he would even contemplate here. And Agathon, what would he become, *want* to become? A philosophic poet? But would such poems really win him the universal fame he yearns for and that Socrates—rather, Diotima promised?

38. Holding and Beholding

Is Diotima's "ladder of love" even a ladder of *love*? She speaks of love in the first three of its six steps, only to replace it with verbs of vision and coupling, "seeing and being-with." But what is this formula but an articulation, an analysis, of the aspects of love? What do lovers do but hold and behold one another?—Can one really do both, though? When lovers embrace, the chin of each rests on the other's shoulder. What do they see? Not one another. Don't they close their eyes? And when they withdraw somewhat and look into each other's eyes, are they holding one another, or are they not at a distance?—Sight and possession, holding and beholding, these two sides to love are not easily reconciled, they are rather in essential tension with one another, but since sight takes priority—Diotima often uses verbs of sight without "being-with"—is possession even possible at the highest level? Can the beautiful itself, the peak of this ladder of "love," really become *mine*? That would be to *defile* it, to violate its purity—

39. *Erōs* and *Poiēsis*

Diotima is compelled to argue that the good is among the objects of *erōs*, and not just that some goods are also beautiful, so that their pursuit might be called properly erotic, but that all human beings love erotically precisely because all human beings want the good—strange, too, since so many goods are utterly ordinary. We don't call the goods of, say, health and hygiene—eating well and brushing our teeth—the objects of erotic longing for good reason, do we? So long as we don't endow them with undue significance, they remain utterly ordinary, mundane, they therefore lack the singularity and transcendence that are so typical of *erōs*. Diotima is well aware, and to "overcome" this insurmountable difficulty, she has to counter ordinary linguistic usage. Unsurprisingly, then, she argues analogically or metaphorically. The term *poiēsis* can refer to "making" of any kind, yet it typically refers to the making of the poet, to "poetry," with all other "makings" given the names of the different arts or crafts, *technai*. And *erōs*? It, too, can refer to "love" of the good and happiness, whatever form it takes, whether as love of exercise or love of wisdom, yet it typically refers to the all-consuming love of the beautiful beloved. All fine and well, but what exactly is the argument of the analogy? What is the relationship between poetry and making, and hence, by analogy, between the beautiful and the good things? Or, to be more precise, since in her examples—the love of exercise and the love of wisdom—Diotima uses a different word for love, a *softer* word, *philia*, what is the relationship between *erōs* and *philia*? Should we re-interpret *philia* on the model of *erōs*, and thus *technē* on the model of *poiēsis*, as Diotima would have it? Or should we rather consider *erōs* from the perspective of *philia*, and thus *poiēsis* from that of *technē*? Or should the terms remain altogether separate? And the spheres analogized? Socrates closes by arguing to Agathon and Aristophanes that he who is a maker of tragedies by art or skill, by *technē*, is also a maker of comedies. He evidently makes a distinction between the poet who makes through inspiration or enthusiasm, the poet as commonly understood, on the one hand, and him who makes through art, the poet of rational production. Like all analogies, Diotima's presents a parallelism where there exists an opposition—here, between rational and technical manipulation of the beautiful, on the one hand, and irrational and enthusiastic absorption into the beautiful, on the other.[16] The young Socrates is persuaded—for the most part, at least. He is just waking up to the disconnect between his concern with beauties and his love of the good things, and he will be fully awake thereto by the end. The mature Socrates knows better.

40. Unanswered Questions

Diotima closes her speech with a series of three questions designed to bring her grand argument to a fittingly grand conclusion. The first sets the stage:

> "Now what do we think," she said, "would happen to someone who sees the beautiful itself distinct, pure, unmixed, not filled up with flesh and colors and any other mortal nonsense, but who can glimpse the divine beautiful itself as of a single form?"

The stage set, the other two questions sketch possible answers. First the pessimistic or, as its advocate might say, realistic answer:

> "Do you think," she said, "life would be a slight thing, when a person looks there and sees and is with that thing, using what he must?"

The third and final question provides the optimistic or, as its detractor might say, unrealistic answer:

> "Or do you take to heart," she said, "that here alone will it happen for him, seeing the beautiful using what makes it visible, to bear not images of virtue, since he does not fix upon an image, but true things, since he fixes upon the truth, and that for him who has borne and nurtured true virtue it falls to become dear to the god and, if for anyone among human beings, immortal, as well?"

It's a highly rhetorical, powerfully emphatic ending to her speech, a stirring climax that the elder Socrates reinforces stylistically by punctuating each question with "she said." And how does young Socrates answer? Does he even answer? We don't know. Why does Socrates omit the outcome? We suspect he never returned to Diotima. And there are good grounds for that. The whole ascent toward immortality requires transcending the particular beautiful things, all of limited beauty, so as to grasp universal beauty, which is in every place, at every time, for every person beautiful; yet we now learn immortality also requires communicating your grasp of universal beauty through virtuous deeds which, in being particular, necessarily lose their universality. So what could ever make us love such offspring, defective as they must be in beauty and thus short as they must fall in delivering on the good, but...the love of our own? Was Diotima's argument against Aristophanes just a tad too hasty, then? It did, at the very least, start us off on this strange venture into abstraction.—At any rate, the mature Socrates does say he is persuaded, but he doesn't say of *what*. After all, what does it mean to be persuaded of unanswered questions? Does it mean that he's persuaded that they're *genuine* questions, questions each of us *must* ask himself? Fine and well. But what about his answer? He says that "for this possession one could not easily get a better co-worker than *erōs*," but what is this unidentified, better, yet harder to find co-worker? And what possession does he mean? The beautiful itself, immortality, or the good things?[17] Which? Amid all this confusion, why no simple, clear, unqualified affirmation that the beautiful itself delivers on its highest promises? Why no enthusiastic affirmation, by young and old Socrates alike, that this life devoted to immortal fame through philosophy is the one life worth living, is *good*? Wouldn't such an affirmation be among "the most beautiful truths" about *erōs*? Would it not, indeed, be the most singularly beautiful of truths? Why *these* omissions?

41. What Did Aristophanes Want to Say?

After Socrates finishes speaking, Aristophanes attempts to engage him in conversation, but we know nothing of what he would have said, thanks to Alcibiades' extravagant entrance. But in poetry the happenstance occurs by design, with a purpose in mind, and thus with some necessity to the whole poem. Alcibiades—his entrance, his speech, even his whole life—takes the place of a conversation between Aristophanes and Socrates: his presence, what he does and says, promises to settle the dispute between the two, or at least to further it. We must turn to Alcibiades.—Still, Plato no doubt also invites us to seek out Aristophanes' response to Socrates, and we might begin by looking to his comic send-up of Socrates, the *Clouds*. There Aristophanes shows Socrates to be too incautious with his teaching, imprudently uttering impieties to foolish men like Strepsiades, who boasts of his "enlightenment" from Socrates and repeats these impieties indiscriminately, even before the money-maker creditors he seeks to defraud and who would therefore have reason to go after the source, Socrates. Did Aristophanes wish to chastise Socrates for imprudence? "But what imprudence? Agathon is no Strepsiades, but quite the opposite, in his ironic dissemblance of his arrogant impieties." I didn't mean Agathon but Aristodemus, in whose presence Socrates denies the divinity of *erōs* and who really ought to have been more tight-lipped. He lets the story circulate among the Socratics, including Apollodorus, who now utters it before some businessmen, who, like their counterparts in the *Clouds*, rely on oaths to the gods, on general *belief* in the gods, for their way of life. "Socrates," Aristophanes may have intended to say, "you and I both know the stuff that gods are made of, the mist and vapors, the smoke the many take to be substantial, but don't be so cavalier with your impieties! You utter them before fools, who then utter them before still greater fools, whose 'philosophic conversion' does nothing for you save provoke a reactionary return to traditional piety, and a *violent* one at that. The city needs these gods, the opinions you submit to vivisection are necessary to its healthy operation, so how do you think things'll turn out, when push comes to shove comes to pitchforks and torches? Whose house will burn down then? Not the temple of the gods, I assure you, but the flimsy walls of your thinkery. Don't cut off your snub nose to spite your face—clean up a little, dress the part!" "But I have!"

42. The Entrance of Alcibiades

Alcibiades waltzes into the gathering with a retinue of attendants and celebrants, festively and handsomely attired, looking very much like the Dionysus who Agathon had promised would judge them in the end. But whose Dionysus is this? That of Euripides' *Bacchae*? Aristophanes' *Frogs*? Or is the answer right in front of us, Plato's *Symposium*? Plato does to Dionysus what Socrates did to Eros: he naturalizes him. It is Alcibiades who finally forces those gathered to drink, whose confessional speech embodies the adage *in vino veritas*, and under whose influence the gathering devolves into a full-blown drinking party, an actual symposium. Plato's "Dionysus," like that of Aristophanes, is the exemplary Athenian, or rather Plato's Alcibiades is the non-comic truth of Aristophanes' Dionysus, an audacious creature of the luxuries and decadence of imperial Athens. And just like Aristophanes' Dionysus with his slave Xanthias, so too Plato's Alcibiades undergoes a humanizing humiliation at the hands of the cunning and capable Socrates, his inferior in social stature but superior in virtue. Socrates accomplishes in deed what Aristophanes could only do in speech, he offered a solution to the problem of Alcibiades that escaped Aristophanes and his Aeschylus and Euripides: you needn't lament the lion cub, nor must you submit to it, for you can *tame* it, should you only succeed in first making yourself a lion tamer.—"Socrates? Tame Alcibiades? How could that be? Was Alcibiades ever tame in *anything* he did, from youth to death? And who else could be blamed for such wild unconventionality but Socrates?" "Cheers to that, and no need to lament or submit here, nor even to tame!"

43. Who Left?

When the revelers burst in at the end of the dialogue, we hear that the door was open because someone had left the gathering—and presumably, because the door was left open, he left in a bit of a huff. Who left, and why? It could, of course, have been someone unnamed. But if not, then who among those named? Alcibiades mentions everyone in his speech, so it must have been either later in the speech or in what followed. Now, we know that Aristodemus, Aristophanes, Agathon, and Socrates are present until morning. That leaves Phaedrus, Pausanias, and Eryximachus. But Aristodemus says that Phaedrus and Eryximachus left only *after* this person's mysterious departure. So only Pausanias is unaccounted for. But why would he leave? Or is it not obvious? Could he really have endured a second more of the flirtatious and erotic game of musical chairs that Socrates and Alcibiades play with his beloved Agathon? He knows how it goes; he's seen it all before. But with Socrates, the ugly, old Socrates? Evidently his education of Agathon in virtue was more of a success than we surmised—too much, even! In any case, for Pausanias this is a bridge too far. He'll have to find another beautiful body.

44. Alcibiades' Speech

"It's about time!" the anonymous comrade must think to himself, having been forced to sit through six speeches about love before getting to the real matter, the business everyone's been talking about: Socrates and Alcibiades. Sure, the story so far has had its moments. Certainly, Aristophanes' hiccups and Agathon's grand display entertained. The comrade was probably even quite shocked at points, if not at Pausanias' slippery self-justification, then certainly at Socrates' explicit denial of Eros' divinity.—Or rather Diotima's, but who's he to split hairs?—But Alcibiades' festive entrance and drunken confession? These are the memorable fodder for gossip. And the contents of that confession, Socrates' effect on him? Much more than gossip, that makes for political intrigue. The comrade's expectations are immediately met: Alcibiades promises to reveal the truth about Socrates, that his praise of love must have been ironic, for he cannot bear to hear Alcibiades praise anyone but himself, Socrates, and that Socrates was this way not just with him but with many of Athens' best youths. That includes Charmides, whose later political career may have lagged behind Alcibiades' for notoriety, but which compensated for that in spades with its bloodiness and brutality. Socrates has a trick, a move, that turns his beloveds into lovers. But how on earth could such an ugly man—a man of the rabble, no less—turn the tables on the best, brightest, and most beautiful sons of the aristocracy? You should probably go read Plato's *Alcibiades* now: it tells the story, or its beginning at least, undistorted by Alcibiades' lens, which shifts variably from red to rosy but never goes completely clear. But the short of it is that Socrates quickly and methodically removed nearly every support for his ambition, convincing him his hopes were unfounded, and thus created a tension in his soul between his desire to be loved by the many and his rational awareness that this desire is, again, unfounded, that it is irrational, and that he ought instead to turn to himself, come to know, care for, and improve himself, before turning to the business of the Athenians. Alcibiades eventually gives in to this irrational desire, but not before attempting to seduce Socrates into spilling his wisdom. It's here that we finally encounter Socrates' hubris. For what is the *Symposium* about but Socrates' hubris, his outrageous arrogance or pride, starting from his rudeness to his gracious host, Agathon, to his shocking impiety in denying the divinity of Eros, among the oldest and hence most venerable of the gods? That's what the comrade has been waiting for all this time, to see Socrates' hubris exposed, naked of his irony.—Now what, according to Alcibiades, is Socrates' hubris? What is the secret, indoor teaching, to which Aristophanes alluded in his *Clouds* but did not reveal? Alcibiades describes a moment so brutally cutting that you can see why Plato made him drunk, for who would confess such a thing but in a moment of drunken candor? Even then it takes Alcibiades some time to work up the courage to make his confession. You can almost *see* him hesitating, stopping himself at tense moments, then urging himself forward with swigs of unmixed wine. He builds slowly, describing the ever-increasing lengths he had to go to in order to seduce Socrates, first hanging around him, next dismissing his attendant, and then stripping and wrestling with him, only to fail each time to consummate. Many times would Socrates decline Alcibiades' invitations to dinner, and though Socrates did eventually accept, he left immediately after they had dined. But when, finally and at long last, Alcibiades succeeded not just in having Socrates to dinner but also in conversing with him long enough that it was too late for him to leave, what happened then?—Alcibiades pauses. He's reluctant to speak. Swig. He doesn't want to reveal Socrates' deed, the *insolent* deed that like a viper's bite struck him in his heart or soul or...—he knows not the word for where, but wherever it struck, strike it did.[18] And the bite? Swig. Alcibiades finally works up the courage to say it. Socrates spent the night. Swig. They reclined beside one another. Under the same blanket. Under Alcibiades' outer robe, too. Swig.—Did he reveal himself further to Socrates, but balk at revealing so much to the others?—Alcibiades then embraced Socrates, and here he reveals that Socrates' bite was...SWIG...a *laugh*. Socrates' hubris was to laugh at something about Alcibiades that Alcibiades took most seriously, something of *his own*, namely, the beauty of his youth, perhaps even in the nude. He could resist the beauty of Alcibiades, even when beholding it directly. Socrates' arrogance turned out to be an uncanny moderation. It was a good that could be found nowhere else in Athens.—"Is this what all the gossip and intrigue was about? *Self-restraint?* What about the impiety, where's the corruption?"—Alcibiades was lost, left wandering, with no reliable path for his ambition, nothing based in a sound understanding of virtue and its requirements. Yet he had, and still has, he claims, unique insight into Socrates' excellence. And he soon acquired, on the battlefield, a sound understanding of its limits. For even when Socrates' excellence became manifest in that most conspicuous place, in the fray of battle, where much is made obvious that would otherwise remain opaque, and even with the additional testimony of Alcibiades himself—even then, all sought to honor not Socrates but Alcibiades. It was in this experience, I believe, that Alcibiades discovered a basis for his ambition. He could do what Socrates never could, likely never would, for Alcibiades was among the few Athenians, perhaps the only, to have glimpsed the vast sea of beauty in Socrates, and he alone among the Socratics had the Athenians so wrapped around his little finger that he could teach them the lessons he had learned, to look down upon the small beauties. He could, in other words, become Socrates' political emissary, a newer, nobler Socrates.—"There's the impiety, there's the corruption! He taught Alcibiades to seek only the loftiest, highest beauties, to pursue an impossibly high transcendence. It was under Socrates' influence that Alcibiades tempted the Athenians to become 'master of the sea' by invading Sicily. Socrates *is* to blame." But Plutarch says Socrates opposed the Sicilian Expedition. And we've seen how far Socrates pushes the beautiful, so far that it begins to break on the shoal of the good things. Let's also not forget that Alcibiades leaves Socrates not his proud emissary but rather in *shame*. Socrates did what no one else in Athens could, not even those who fought hardest against her decadence, and against Socrates, as well: he made Alcibiades blush.

45. Alcibiades after Socrates

Alcibiades' later political career, after the wars he fought with Socrates, is both fascinating and frightening, and we turn to it now with a healthy dose of trepidation, cautious not to fall prey to the gossip and intrigue that have surrounded it since the dialogue began, and sensitive especially to the bearing it has on Socrates and one's judgment of him. Alcibiades' early encounters with Socrates left Alcibiades nearly broken in two, pulled toward the Athenians, on the one hand, whom he both loves and contemns, and toward Socrates, on the other, whom he reveres as a god—not to say obeys, of course, for like Agathon with Pausanias, Alcibiades cannot bear to grow old, sitting idly beside Socrates. This troubling, psychic rift remains even these many years later, in Agathon's house. It persists until his end, his life a sort of silent dialogue of these two parts with one another. *Ecce homo*:

This evening, in the gathering at Agathon's, Alcibiades is on the cusp of his first major political victory. He will soon persuade the Athenians to invade Sicily and to let him lead the expedition—or rather *co*-lead it. A political victory followed by a double betrayal, the Athenians of Alcibiades, and Alcibiades of the Athenians. His subsequent exile and wandering finds him aiding Athens' enemies—first Sparta, then Persia—as he wrestles with the mixture of love and contempt he bears towards his fellow citizens. Was this Socrates' effect? He did make himself Alcibiades' god. It was that strange Socrates, the ugly, shoeless Socrates, whom we've now learned denied Eros' divinity and who replaced the traditional worship of the gods through priests and prophets with *philosophy*. Philosophy, he tells us, or rather Diotima tells us—but who's actually paying attention?—is the perfect end of *erōs*, here understood as culminating in the love of honor. This love is not easily satisfied with the limited bounds of time and place, nor the borders of cities, but stretches out beyond them toward the universal; such honor therefore demands of its lovers a flexibility in speech and deed rarely found among the rigid habits and conventions that determine more conventional lovers of honor, to say nothing of the anonymous majority of mankind. And what is Alcibiades if not flexible, this man who blended in so easily in Athens, Sparta, and Persia? And also Socrates, who, depending on the company he presently keeps, readily becomes whatever he must, whether an Achillean gadfly or midwife to pregnant boys? Socrates' fingerprints are all over the scene of the crime.—

Such might be the reaction of the comrade, or those in his situation. But it stops too short in Alcibiades' career, too short in its understanding of Socrates, as well. In conversation, Socrates always becomes what he must, and before those beautiful talents like Alcibiades, who also love having lovers, Socrates must become the most demanding lover, mirroring back to them a still higher contempt, a contempt for their natural gifts. What makes their other lovers sacrifice so much for Alcibiades must be, for Socrates, a paltry thing, a negligible gift, in light of all that he possesses—in light of his *virtue*. But what might Alcibiades glean from Socrates' posturing, if effective? He would find in Socrates a sublime moderation, in his resisting a man so beautiful and so chary with his love as to be commonly known as the beloved *par excellence*. Alcibiades would, as he says, become the lover and thus see in Socrates the highest demand a beloved could make of his lovers, that they be truly worthy of reciprocation, but on a level Phaedrus never could have imagined. And he would see further that, for all his natural gifts, he would nevertheless lack this virtue that belongs uniquely to Socrates. Of course, Socrates showed him, too, that this virtue was not among Alcibiades' natural gifts and that he would therefore have to work to acquire it. But it had long been the vice of Alcibiades to flit from one "lover" to the next, also to seek out the path of least resistance, and in the wake of Socrates' attempt to educate him Alcibiades reverted to his old behavior. Nevertheless, his later experience with the many would soon teach Alcibiades the truth of Socrates' arguments, as he came to learn firsthand how fickle lovers can be, how suddenly they can turn on their beloveds, that Socrates was therefore right to demand more of Alcibiades, and that he himself, like Socrates, ought not to succumb to such lovers but rather work to make them better. And so Alcibiades did, when years later, after a long exile, the Athenian army fighting in Samos asked him to return from exile and lead them back to Athens to reverse an oligarchic revolution and restore the democratic party into power. What a temptation! It promised to bring Alcibiades back into Athens' good graces, removing the suspicion of aspirations to tyranny, as the crimes of sacrilege had led the people to fear, and rather proving him the great savior of the democracy. But he resisted this temptation, insisting instead on a more mixed, moderate, or just form of government that reconciled the interests of the democratic and oligarchic factions, the regime of the so-called Five Thousand. During his time, Thucydides declared, Athens never had a better regime. Cautious as to the vices of his lovers, the Athenian *dēmos*, Alcibiades resisted the temptation to gratify them; he rather guided them to be better, because more moderate in their ambitions, and thus worthy of their beloved Alcibiades. There's more than a hint here of the moderation Alcibiades saw in Socrates. Such a regime would have pleased Aristotle, at least.[19] And Socrates? Plutarch reports, again, that he did not support the Sicilian Expedition, and there Alcibiades had behaved in a wholly contrary manner toward his lovers than with the army at Samos.

Only a few years later, however, Alcibiades fell once again to the temptation to beautify, even divinize, himself, rather than ennoble Athens. He saw an opportunity in the procession to Eleusis, which had not been conducted by land for many years, but rather by sea, owing to Spartan occupation of the Dekeleia, the region of Attica through which the procession would typically pass. The opportunity was twofold for Alcibiades. This was the very procession whose mysteries he had been accused of profaning, an accusation that in turn led to his escape from capital punishment and his defection to the enemy. And it was thanks to his aid, as a defector, that the Spartans had taken the Dekeleia in the first place. It was, in other words, an opportunity to make amends on both counts, by showing himself a friend to the democracy and the gods at once. And so he did: to the amazed eyes of all the Athenians watching, the Spartans did not interfere with the procession, which had the effect, Plutarch claims, of turning popular support in favor of Alcibiades—in favor of making him *tyrant*. His self-divinization came with great risks, then, and ultimately with a great cost. For, after Alcibiades' failure at Notion, the people turned against him, either for his negligence or out of suspicion of subterfuge. Plutarch, always so insightful on

Alcibiades, summarizes his error perfectly:

> If anyone, it was Alcibiades who seems to have been undone by his own reputation. For it was great and brimming with daring and cunning, the sources of his success, his failures bringing him suspicion, as though he feigned them (*ou spoudasantos*), since his lack of ability was met with distrust. For whenever he pursued a thing seriously (*spoudasanta*), *nothing* could escape him.

Save Socrates, of course. Alcibiades succumbed to his lovers, so Socrates stayed away. He knew better.

Alcibiades subsequently left Athens once again, but this time he did not wait for the Athenians to convict him, rather he went away of his own accord. He walked away from his lovers but not to his beloved Socrates. He had to stay away from Athens, and Socrates seldom left the city's walls. What little hope there may have been of reconciliation was now gone. And there they died.—

But what about Socrates after Alcibiades? We venture here still further beyond our dialogue, but let's indulge a word or two. Socrates knew to stay away, but he seems to have learned this lesson too late. It only took one conversation, many years before the *Symposium*, for their reputations to be inextricably linked. At the end of that conversation, Socrates worried and remarked, "It is not because I distrust anything in your nature, but because I see the strength of the city, that I fear it will overpower me and you." His final words here are *sou kratēsē*: it is a serious warning of the city's power that playfully puns on Socrates' *name*. It would eventually take a poet of Plato's immense skill and wisdom to rehabilitate this reputation.

46. The Poets and the Philosopher Converse

Aristodemus wakes up, and through his sleepy eyes and ears, and foggy brain, manages to preserve the last and highest moment in the contest of wisdom between poetry and philosophy, a shred of an argument really, a mere proposition, a claim, of which Socrates persuades the poets, to wit, "that knowing how to make comedy and tragedy belongs to the same man, and that he who is a maker of tragedies by art or skill is also a maker of comedies." What was Socrates' argument for this claim? Plato is silent, or rather he speaks in such moments only through the drama. Here, first Aristophanes, then Agathon drifts away, overcome by drink and exhaustion, while Socrates dusts himself off and goes about his day as usual. Socrates is in full control of himself, while Aristophanes and Agathon, to different degrees, succumb to outside forces. Is this what Socrates means by the man who makes tragic poems by art or skill, by *technē*? Full control of oneself gives one full control of what one makes, of one's poems? Averse to reproduction, Socrates nevertheless understands it and knows the sort of poet he's looking for—but what *is* he looking for? We sense, at least, what he *isn't* looking for. Aristophanes failed to enchant the group, no one would take his Zeus seriously. What gods he can make are laughable, *ridiculous*.[20] He's in control but lacks the necessary ability. Yet still he tries, so how in control is he?—In any case, the argument does not speak to him: it concerns rather "the maker of *tragedies* by art," and that's beyond his ken. Such a life is, however, available to Agathon, though one wonders whether he'd ever make comedies, whether he'd be willing to write verses ugly, shameful, ridiculous to the many, whether, conversely, he's too wrapped up in the theater, that is, in the praise of the *dēmos*. Remember how he spoke: genuflection to a god, whose divinity Socrates openly denied. Agathon saw in his feminine seduction of the people a power to pacify the warlike, to overcome them, and he called that manliness, while Socrates' fear proved his cowardice. But we knew even then that his speech was no pacification. And we know now, too, that his irony evinces not a superlative manliness but a lack thereof, that making new gods risks incurring notoriety, infamy, and death, and that Socrates accepts that risk, pays the highest price, but reaps the greatest reward, the reputation as "the turning-point and vortex of so-called world history." Socratic philosophy is more fundamentally *manly* than the effete Agathon could ever appreciate. His failure is shown not so much in anything he says, for he says very little after Socrates' speech, but in what he does, turning toward the beautiful Alcibiades, beloved to the *dēmos*, and away from the conversation between Socrates and Aristophanes. It's a cruel bit of irony that Agathon has been immortalized not for his plays but as a minor character in the works of that poet who would take his place seated beside Socrates, in the works of Plato. Agathon may mock the people, but he loves their affection too much, he seeks fame through them too much to profane so openly their gods, the gods of the city, to do what Socrates has done, to the shock of the comrade and the Athenian people, to do what Plato would go on to do, and consecrate Socrates as a new hero, the Achilles of the contemplative life. And the gods? Here Plato's silence is deafening.

47. Socrates at Dawn

Socrates leaves just as he entered—solitary, mysterious, and thinking to himself, doted on and observed from a distance by his lover, then Agathon and now Aristodemus. He is the sole survivor of this gathering of notables, an evening which will live in infamy. There can be no mistake, Socrates has left his mark on this gathering, on all in it. Nietzsche put it best:

> According to Plato's description, he left the *Symposium* at daybreak as the last of the revelers, to begin a new day; yet around him, on the benches and on the floor, the sleeping table-mates remained behind, to dream of Socrates, the true erotic.[21]

He and Phaedrus will speak again before too long, and Pausanias won't soon get over the sight of his beautiful beloved flirting with the ugly old Socrates. Eryximachus surely enjoys the philosophical-medical hybrid Socrates offered him, while the poets are left to puzzle over Socrates' new and mysterious vision of their respective genres united under a single art. The worst lot surely falls to Alcibiades, who will wake up and remember his drunken confession, if it doesn't already dog him on the way home, only to be filled with shame, perhaps even rage, that his secret escaped his lips. And we cannot, of course, neglect Aristodemus amid all these leading lights of Athens, small and forgettable as he may be, for it is through his ears that we hear all we've heard and through his eyes that we watch Socrates depart. He, too, will not soon forget this evening but will tell the story for years to come, and it will grow famous among his fellow lovers of Socrates, these Socratics. But what about Socrates? What effect did this gathering have on him? Unlike Dionysus, he leaves this home without a poet, but does he leave at least with a lesson? He does learn what sort of poet he doesn't need; he may even learn what sort he does. And he will meet him, Plato, before too long. It will be not the least of the good things in Socrates' life.

48. Inside and Outside

We're about to leave the *Symposium*, to venture outside its bounds, so here is as good a place as any to say a thing or two about the repeated motif of inside vs. outside. What happens inside? Agathon's charming dinner, the praises of *erōs*, and Alcibiades' praise of Socrates, as well as the celebration of the birth of Aphrodite, Alcibiades' attempt to seduce Socrates, and the blissful slumber of the leading lights of Athens and the late-come revelers. And what happens outside? Poverty's intercourse with Plenty and Socrates at war, but above all the silent meditation of Socrates on the porch of Agathon's neighbor. Socrates came inside on his own terms, and rather disruptively. In his reluctance to enter, he is the very opposite of Alcibiades and, later, the revelers, eager to be a part of the festivities at Agathon's house. The gathering finally devolves into a Bacchic revelry, a literal intoxication following the metaphoric intoxication of the speeches that preceded it. "Inside" seems, in *this* text, to represent intoxication with the beautiful, while "outside" seems to represent love of the good things. Or perhaps it stands rather for the limits that the necessary places on the beautiful and, consequently, the modesty of the good things, the homely and not-so-sexy goods available to us. For not every good is devoid of beauty, is it? Nature does supply, after all, lovely olive groves, beside which one might gather with friends and converse.

49. Plato

Plato's *Drinking Party* is over. Let's dust ourselves off, survey the scene, assess the damage—above all to ourselves. How easy is it for readers, how easy has it been for us, or for me at least, to let this vintage intoxicate, though as an intricate puzzle might, consuming one's attention while having in addition an ever-sobering core. How did Plato manage to combine the highest intoxication with the highest sobriety, how did he succeed in rendering his teacher's mixture of hubris and moderation, so active and adaptable, into the stubbornly immobile written word? Upon meeting Socrates, we have been told, he burned his tragedies, and beneath his pillow on his deathbed was found a worn copy of the plays of Aristophanes. In these two facts, apocryphal or not, are distilled to its essence the whole of Plato's art of writing: the ability, the talent even, to charm the multitude, spurned then transposed to the decidedly *un*popular activity of scrutinizing the claims men make about themselves and their world—all on the one hand, and on the other: the ability to see all that is ridiculous in what men commonly revere, to extract therefrom the kernel of seriousness amid all this chaff, in short, to rise to those heights of the soul, seen from which even tragedy ceases to have tragic effects. The tragedy of men with noble aspirations, based on their venerable or common opinions, venerable yet misguided about their limitations, common and therefore limited in their precision and application—their tragedy turns, under the scrutiny of Socratic dialectics, into a satyr play, if not an outright comedy. It's here that the basic questions begin to shine their light, to illuminate the comedy and tragedy of life. How does Plato do all this? He clearly holds the key, the argument Socrates presented the poets but which is lost to us; he is, as we've long surmised, the poet Socrates sought, who is by art a maker of tragedies and could become, *did* become a maker of comedies. Aristodemus, who falls so short in his imitation of Socrates, lacks his idol's endurance and, drowsy with drink, spills all but the most essential of beans. Couldn't Plato have done otherwise? Or isn't his secrecy here a subtle self-revelation, that unlike Apollodorus, Aristodemus, and Alcibiades, unlike these lovers of Socrates, he knew when to speak and when to be silent? Does he not reveal that he learned this from Aristophanes, who never stoops so low as to bring Socrates' most private lessons onto the stage? What Plato suggests is that by combining the way of Socrates with the way of Aristophanes, he avoided the conflict with the vulgar and thus the fate of Socrates. It somehow escaped the notice of the Athenians—and, in the two and a half millennia since, of many others besides—that he, too, was guilty of making new gods. What might those gods be?

Notes

1 172b2 (*sundeipnō*), 172a7 (*sunousian*), 172b7 (*sunousia*), 172c1 (*sunousian*), 173b3 (*sunousia*); 174a6 (*deipnon*), 174b1 (*deipnon*), 174b4 (*daitas*), 174c2 (*hestiōntos*), 174c3 (*thoinēn*), 174c7 (*thoinēn*), 174e4 (*deipnein*), 174e6 (*sundeipnēsēs*), 174e11 (*deipnon*), 175b5 (*hestiate*), 175b8 (*deipnon*), 175c6 (*deipnountas*), 175e10 (*deipnon*), 176a2 (*deipnēsantos*); 176a4 (*poton*), 176a6 (*piometha*), 176a7 (*potou*), 176b1 (*pinoimen*), 176b4 (*poseōs*), 176b4 (*bebaptismenōn*), 176b7 (*pinein*), 176c3 (*pinein*), 176c6–7 (*pinein oinon*), 176c7 (*methuskesthai*), 176d2 (*methē*), 176d3 (*piein*), 176d4 (*kraipalōnta*).

2 Pausanias seems to drink (see 181a1). Aristophanes' hiccups suggest he does, as well, but hiccups occur no less for drinking than for not drinking (see 185c5–7, also note 13 below). In his speech, Agathon refers to their gathering as a *sunodos* and *sunousia*, implying that still, at this late stage, not everyone is drinking (197d2). When Alcibiades enters, he pours wine for Socrates, so his cup was empty, though we don't know why—in any case, it only then that Aristodemus explicitly says that Socrates drinks (214a2–3, 6). Only at the very end, after the speeches are done and a group of revelers has stormed in, does everyone drink wine to excess (223b5–6). Consider, too, 212c8–d2 with 213e7–8, 214c7–8, 222c3–4.

3 Consider 172b5–6.

4 *Phaedo* 60a3–b1.

5 On this and similar points, I owe much to Benardete's essay on the *Symposium*.

6 See 212c6–d5, 213a3–b3, 223b1–6.

7 The artist has declined to receive credit for his work.

8 *Love and Friendship* (Simon & Schuster, 1993), 478 (emphasis added).

9 Apollodorus and Alcibiades each mention philosophy twice, while Pausanias mentions it thrice. Socrates mentions it nine times, though eight of those are as Diotima and only one as himself—and even then, only as his younger self.

10 Consider Kant, *Kritik der Urteilskraft* §8 (end) in light of *Hippias Major* 294c8–d4.

11 Xenophon, *Memorabilia* I.4. Compare §30.

12 See Plato, *Cleitophon*.

13 Compare 189c4 and 190c8 with 206a1. See, also, 220c6, 221d2.

14 Consider 218e2–219a2.

15 See the entry for *aei* in Liddell, Scott, Jones, and McKenzie, *A Greek-English Lexicon* (Oxford University Press, 1940).

16 See Benardete, "On Plato's *Phaedo*" 282 in *The Argument of the Action* (University of Chicago Press, 2000). Compare 180.

17 A reference to 205a1. This is essential to understanding the proper order of Socrates' speech.

18 See Leo Strauss, *On Plato's* Symposium, 242–43 with *The City and Man* (University of Chicago Press, 1964), 61–62.

19 *Politics* IV.11.

20 See paragraph 11 of my forthcoming essay, "Leo Strauss's Intention with Plato's *Symposium*."

21 See Nietzsche, *Kritische Studienausgabe*, ed. Colli and Montinari (De Gruyter, 1999), I:91, ll. 20–33.

Acknowledgements

Those companions from whom I've learned something about the topics covered in the *Symposium* are too many to name. But I must express gratitude above all to my two close friends, Gregory McBrayer and David Bahr. The two met at the University of Maryland, where the former was a graduate student in political philosophy, already advanced in years, and the latter an undergraduate, young, handsome, and eager to learn. I would befriend David only a few years later at St. John's College, and soon Greg, as well. But their lasting friendship, especially in the reciprocity of their playful banter and mutual assistance, was and continues to be a model of lifelong companionship. Relevant for this volume are a series of conversations the three of us recorded and released through our podcast, *The New Thinkery*, thanks to the generous assistance of our producer, Jake Gannon. Those conversations were instrumental in massaging the developing thoughts that have here reached maturity; for the benefit of their friendly conversation, I am grateful. Greg also assisted in acquiring the art found on page 29. I am grateful likewise to Justin Gottschalk, who read and commented on an earlier version of the first twenty-six sections, and Lewis Slawsky, for his helpful editorial advice. All errors are, of course, my own. Though with friends like these, one always worries that their "benefactions" could hide a bit of playful cruelty.